Edward Arber, John Udall

A Demonstration of the Truth of that Discipline, which Christ has Prescribed in His Word...

Edward Arber, John Udall

A Demonstration of the Truth of that Discipline, which Christ has Prescribed in His Word...

ISBN/EAN: 9783744670982

Printed in Europe, USA, Canada, Australia, Japan

Cover: Foto ©Lupo / pixelio.de

More available books at **www.hansebooks.com**

The English Scholar's Library of Old and Modern Works

[REV. JOHN UDALL]

A Demonstration of the truth

of that Discipline, which CHRIST hath prescribed in His Word, for the government of His Church, in all times and places until the end of the world

[July—November 1588]

EDITED BY

EDWARD ARBER

F.S.A. ETC. LATE EXAMINER IN ENGLISH
LANGUAGE AND LITERATURE
TO THE UNIVERSITY OF
LONDON

WESTMINSTER

ARCHIBALD CONSTABLE AND CO.

1895

(All rights reserved)

CONTENTS.

	PAGE
Bibliography	vi
Introduction	vii–xii

A Demonstration of the truth of that Discipline &c. ... 1
TO THE SUPPOSED GOVERNORS OF THE CHURCH OF ENGLAND &c. ... 3
TO THE READER ... 8

A Demonstration of Discipline ... 8

CHAP.
1. The Word of GOD describeth perfectly the lawful Form of Church Government, and the Officers that are to execute the same: from which no Christian Church ought to swerve ... 13
2. Every Office in the Church must have express Scriptural authority for it; and no one is to be appointed to such Office unless it be previously vacant ... 17
3. Church Officers cannot be non-resident ... 25
4. The appointment of Officers rests with the Church, and not with patrons 29
5. The Eldership is to thoroughly examine all persons previous to their appointment to Office in the Church ... 34
6. No man to be admitted to Church Office until by sufficient trial and due examination he is found by the Eldership to be fit ... 36
7. Every Church Officer is to be ordained by the laying on of hands ... 40
8. Such ordaining to be done with humble prayer on the part of the Eldership and the Congregation ... 42
9. The value of the Laying on of hands ... 43
10. There should be one Bishop or Pastor president over every Congregation. All such Pastors to be of equal authority ... 44
11. In each Congregation, there should be a Doctor; which is an Office different from that of a Pastor ... 49
12. Every Congregation should have Elders, to see into the manners of the people; and to be assistant unto the Minister in the ecclesiastical government ... 50
13. In every Congregation, there should be certain Deacons attending to money matters ... 55
14. There should be, perpetually, in every Congregation, an Eldership; consisting of (1) the Pastor or Pastors; (2) Doctor, if there be any; and (3) Elders: to govern the same ... 58
15. Church Government is only spiritual: therefore its Governors may not meddle in civil causes or secular affairs ... 67
16. The placing and displacing of Church Officers appertains unto the Eldership ... 71
17. Public Admonition is very profitable and necessary; and is to be given by the Eldership ... 73
18. When Admonition fails, the Eldership may exclude from the Lord's Supper; and, in the case of Officers, suspend the same ... 75
19. Where both Admonition and Suspension fail: the Eldership may excommunicate ... 78

The Conclusion of the whole book ... 82

[In some copies of the original, the following, on an inserted fly-leaf, is found.]

A Table of Discipline, the particular heades whereof, are handled in the seueral chapters, according to the number wherevvith they are noted: as follovveth

The Discipline of the Church is, the order that GOD hath prescribed in his worde, for the ruling of the same: cap. 1. The offices and officers of whiche, are to bee considered in	General, the calling,	wherevnto, to wit, to		A certaine office, Chap. 2
				Execute his office fayrhfully, Chap. 3
		how it must be, by	Election; whiche must be done by.	The people, chap. 4.
				Examination, chap. 5.
				Consent (onely) to a man fit for the place, Chap. 6.
			Ordination	By whom it must be: by the eldership, Chap. 7.
				The maner howe, by { publike prayer with the people, chap. 8. / laying on of hands, cap. 9.
	Particular, the officers and officers,	Simple, by themselues.	Byshops.	Pastours, chap. 10 / Doctours, chap. 11.
			Deacons or Church seruants	Ouerseers, chap. 12 / Distributers, chap. 13.
		Compound, the Synod Ecclesiasticall,	What	Be the parties: Pastours, Doctours, and Elders, Chap. 14. / Is the authoritie thereof, chap. 15.
			Wherein it consisteth: in	placing and displacing; chap. 16. / Censures by { word, chap. 17. / deed { suspention, cap. 18 / Excommunication, chap. 19.

BIBLIOGRAPHY.

ISSUE IN THE AUTHOR'S LIFETIME.

1. [July-November 1588, East Molesey, Surrey.] See title at *p.* 1.

∴ This Work occasioned *A Remonstrance: or plaine detection of some of the faults . . . . cobled up together in a Booke, entituled,* A Demonstration *&c.* London. 1590.

ISSUE SINCE HIS DEATH.

2. 2 August 1880. Willesden, London, N.W. The present impression.

∴ *All as separate publications.*

INTRODUCTION.

HERE is nothing more heart-rending than judicial murder for ecclesiastical opinions ; when men of the highest personal integrity and spotless citizenship come to their end unrighteously, either by long imprisonment or by swift execution. It is one of the glories of Queen VICTORIA's reign, that no one has suffered therein the extreme penalty of the law, for any simple political offence ; much more, for ecclesiastical matters. Yet, solely for *DIOTREPHES* and this *Demonstration*, JOHN UDALL, an absolutely upright and pure-minded man, was cut off in the prime of life, a victim to the secular power and political influence of Queen ELIZABETH's Bishops.

Thus these two books must, necessarily, excite a deep interest in all who have a true sympathy with human nature ; as being among the number of those works which have proved to be the death warrants of their authors. It does not appear that UDALL in any single *act*, disobeyed the law of the land ; or even the injunctions of the High Commission. He had nothing to do with the Martinist publications, except that he gave PENRY certain notes as to matters of fact which had transpired. He repudiated altogether the Martinist use of satire and invective in the advancement of the common Cause he had so dearly at heart. He was universally respected by all the earnest men of the time : and even by such a man as JAMES I. Nowadays, so far from being imprisoned to death, he would have become one of the Leaders of Opinion in the nation.

It is but another illustration of the strong-handed Episcopal control of the press at that time, that such an Ecclesiastical Epitome as this, had to be secretly printed in an out-of-the-way village.

INTRODUCTION.

As we have seen in the *Introductory Sketch, pp.* 89, 115, this *Demonstration* was set up in type by ROBERT WALDEGRAVE at Mistress CRANE's country house at East Molesey, near Hampton Court. It was set in a small size of Roman and Italic type, which WALDEGRAVE had managed to save in a box under his cloak on the 13th May 1588, when his press, printing *DIOTREPHES*, was seized; and which he left in the charge of Mistress CRANE for about two months. This type, which the London printers well knew as WALDEGRAVE's type, was evidently cast on the Continent, as the semicolon so frequently occurs in this Text. At that time, that stop was not usually cast in English founts of type; neither was it recognized as a stop at all, by such a critic as GEORGE PUTTENHAM in his description of English Punctuation in his *Arte of Poesie*, which was entered at Stationers' Hall for publication on the 9th November 1588; that is, about the very time this *Demonstration* was first coming into secret circulation.

It was comparatively easy to get the manuscript into type, though the occasional errors of spelling are a witness of its troublesomeness: but the supreme difficulty was to machine it. All the hand-printing presses of London were registered. No one could own one, but a fully qualified member of the Stationers' Company; and most of these were only allowed one. In some way or other, probably through WALDEGRAVE, PENRY bought a press; all Orders, Injunctions, &c., of the High Commission and the Stationers' Company to the contrary notwithstanding: and, apparently, he, himself, helped WALDEGRAVE to work off the sheets here reprinted. As the supply of type was very scanty, one sheet was probably set and worked off at a time; and then the type distributed for the composition of a fresh one. The original is on a much smaller page than the present one; to save paper, and to facilitate the secret distribution.

About three weeks were occupied in printing this book; and *during those three weeks* the Spanish Armada was sailing for the English Channel.

Mistress CRANE's servant, NICHOLAS TOMKINS, swore on the 15th February 1589, that PENRY and WALDEGRAVE were "about 3 weeks in her Howse in the Country after Midsommer [1588]." *Introductory Sketch, p.* 85. *Ed.* 1879. But WALDEGRAVE's movements in that neighbourhood had already excited suspicions. In the *Stationers' Registers* are recorded the following payments.

Item, paid the xth of June [1588] for a Dynner when bothe the wardens [F. COLDOCK and H. CONNEWAY], master WATKYNS, and master DENHAM, and the Pursuyvant, with JOHN WOLF, THOMAS STRANGE, and THOMAS DRAPER wente to Kingston. iiijs ijd/

Item the same mens supper at Kingston	xs vjd/
Item to the poore woman whose house was serched at Kingston	ijs/
Item the boatehire to and from Kingston	xiiijs/
Item for twooe lynckes the same tyme	viijd/
Item for a warrant for PENRYE and NORTHE goinge and comminge by water [*i.e.*, *to Lambeth Palace*] to get yt signed.	iijs viijd/
Item paid to WATSON the Pursuyvant the same tyme for goinge to Kingston.	xs

Transcript &c., I. 528. *Ed.* 1875.[1]

So the entire trip cost the Stationers' Company £2 5s., or about £13 in present money. MARTIN MARPRELATE has given us a vivid picture of this expedition.

And I would wish the Purcivants and the Stacioners / with the Woolfe their beadle / not to be so redy to molest honest men. And Stacioners / I would wish you not to be so francke with your bribes / as you were to Thomas Draper / I can tell you his grace had need to prouide a bag ful of Items for you / if you be be so liberal. Were you so foolish (or so malicious against Walde-graue) to give that knaue Draper fiue pounds to betray him into your wretched hands : he brought you to Kingstone vpon Thames / with Purcivants to take him / where he should be a printing books in a Tinkars house. (your selues being disguised so / that Walde-graue might not know you / for of Citizens you were becom(e) ruffians) There you were to seek that could not be found / and many such iournies may you make. But when you came to London / you laid Thomas Draper in the Counter for cosenage. O well bowlde / when Iohn of London throwes his bowle / he will runne after it / and crie rub / rub / rub / and say the diuill go with thee. *Epistle, pp.* 38, 39. *Ed.* 1880.

After this search, PENRY and WALDEGRAVE went further into the country, to East Molesey ; and there produced this book in the beginning of July. It came abroad with the *Epistle*, in the beginning of November 1588 : and, curiously enough, the present reprints of both works will be published on the same day, nearly three hundred years later.

II.

His piece of Presbyterian Argumentation was written, when the Controversy to which it relates was at a white heat. All other possible means had already been taken; but without effect.

We haue sought to aduaunce this cause of God, by humble suit to the parliamente, by supplication to your Conuocation house, by writing in defence of it, and by challenging to dispute for it, seeing none of these means vsed by vs haue preuailed. *p.* 7.

The Bishops had done nothing, and would do nothing. These Reformers were so thoroughly confident they were in the right, that they even dared to say

Venture your byshopprickes vpon a disputation, and wee will venture our liues, take the challenge if you dare: if the truth be on your side, you may hereby, be restored to your dignities, and be no more troubled by vs: but if the trueth be against you, what shal it profit you to win the whole world, and afterward loose your own souls. *pp.* 6, 7.

To understand aright, UDALL's purpose and standpoint; we should consider three things.

1. The Bishops' passive resistance, of which Lord BACON complained in his *Advertisement*. See *Introductory Sketch, pp.* 146-168.

2. There were, at this time, no Dissenters in England: and only a few Brownists in Holland. Every Protestant Englishman belonged to the Church of England, whether he would or not. The right to constitute a Protestant Ecclesiastical Society (on however sound an orthodoxical basis) in the Kingdom, outside the Church of England, was stiffly and absolutely denied; and all attempts thereat rigorously suppressed. No one could throw off the authority of the Bishops; who considered Conformity and Orthodoxy as inseparable from Loyalty and Patriotism. At what infinite trouble have these since been disentangled!

Nor was this a matter of mere mental assent. The Bishops, as Ordinaries, were the Rulers of the Church: and the iniquities of the Spiritual Courts of that time are not yet fully recognized and understood by us.

3. Personally, it was a struggle between the Bishops alone, and the best of the Clergy and Laity banded together against them. Technically, it

was a fight between the Episcopacy and the Eldership: but inasmuch as the Eldership rested on popular election, it was really a conflict between Official Power and Public Opinion.

The Prelates were in possession. For their every act, they could plead either legal enactment, or an hitherto unchallenged prescription. Besides having all the written law on their side; they were Judges themselves, with large and not strictly-defined powers. They commanded the services of a small army of rapacious officials, who were ever at their beck and call. Add to these things, their temporalities and great wealth, their peerage, their supposed spiritual power; and were they not immoveable! Were a few ecclesiastical Radicals, small people altogether, to rise up against them, and bring them to judgement? Well, that is exactly what UDALL and his friends tried to do. They endeavoured to bring these mighty men to the bar of public opinion. Of course, these pioneers were destroyed in the attempt: but their ideas remained and fructified, until the Long Parliament at last swept away the whole Episcopal system.

III.

HE intention of the Writer of this *Demonstration*, was that it should be a kind of Ecclesiastical *EUCLID* of Church Management: and nowhere else do we get, in so short a space, such a clear tracing of the precise rift, in matters of Public Worship and Church Order, between the two systems of the Episcopacy and the Eldership, as they subsisted in ELIZABETH's reign.

Doctor BRIDGES, in his *Defence &c.*, 1587, describes the Presbyterian Government as a Tetrarchy of Doctor, Pastor, Elders and Deacons: but according to this Scheme of Organization, the Deacons had no share in the Eldership. *p.* 58.

UDALL's process herein, is that of a rigid Logic. He asserts for the Eldership a prescription, *in all times and places until the End of the World.* Then comes the irony of History in regard to such confident dogmatizing. As a matter of fact, the Holy Discipline, in its integrity, and as here defined by UDALL, did not last two generations in England.

From the Eldership, the Doctor disappeared very soon; and the Pastors therein were, as soon, reduced to one. When the Pilgrim Fathers moved from Amsterdam to Leyden in 1609 under their single Pastor, the Rev. JOHN ROBINSON, they chose, *MASTER BREWSTER, Assistant to him, in the place of an Elder* [See *English Garner, Vol. II. p.* 365, *Ed.* 1879]. So that the Elders also, in that famous Community, had been reduced to one; and this, within about twenty years of the writing of this Text, wherein UDALL claims for the Eldership, in its completeness, that it is a divinely-ordained Fixture until the end of the world. WILLIAM BREWSTER lived till 1644 as the Ruling Elder of the Pilgrim Church: and it may be fairly questioned whether he did not altogether outlive the whole Institution of the Eldership, as it is laid down and defined in this text.

This but one side of the picture of those times : the other the Prelatical side will occupy us in our study of the Martinist tracts. Meanwhile, one clear distinction lies on the surface. If the Eldership was severe, narrow-minded, or harsh ; yet it was never corrupt. There was integrity of life in it. But the Episcopal system contained much moral corruption, and was often monstrously tyrannical.

A DEMONSTRATION OF
the trueth of that Discipline which *Christe hath prescribed in his worde for* the gouernement of his Church, in all times and places, vntill the ende of the worlde.

¶ Wherein are gathered into a plaine *forme of reasoning, the proofes thereof; out* of the scriptures, the euidence of it by the light of reason rightly ruled, and the testimonies that haue beene giuen therevnto, by the course of the Churche certaine hundreths of yeares after the Apostles time; and the generall consent of the Churches rightly reformed in these latter times: according as they are alleaged and maintained, in those seuerall bookes that haue bin written concerning the same.

MATTH. 21. 38.
The husbandmen said among themselues, this is the heire; come let vs kill him, and let vs take his inheritaunce.

LVKE. 19. 27.
Those mine enemies which would not that I shoulde raigne ouer them, bring hither, and slea them before me

¶ TO THE SVPPOSED GOUERNOURS

of the Church of England, the Archbyshops,
lord Byshops, Archdeacons, and the
rest of that order.

Anie and most euident haue our declarations bin concerning the truth of that gouerment, which Christ hath prescribed in his word for the ruling of the Church; which we haue manifested vnto you, both by our writinges and speches, as occasion hath bin offered: neuer hath any one of you taken in hand to saye any thing against it, but it hath made his eyes to dazzle, as the clearest sun-shining; wherby he hath beene driuen to wander hyther and thyther, groping for euasions, and yet coulde not escape, but hath fallen into infinite most monstrous absurdities, and blasphemous assertions, (as by their writinges yet extant it may appeare) so forcible is the trueth, to amaze the gaine-sayers thereof, and so pregnant is falsehood to beget and bring forth thousands of absurdities, and euery one worse then other. And will you still continue in your damnable, and most deuellish course? Haue you solde your selues vnto Sathan, to fight for him vntill you be dampned in Hell with him? Haue you morgaged the saluation of your soules and bodies, for the present fruition of your pompe and plesure, is it because you see not what you should do? It may be so, for many are so blinde, that they grope euen at noone day; but me thinkes it can hardly be so, vnlesse you be they that haue eyes and see not, for the cause hath bene (by the

blessing of God) so managed, that many ploughmen, artificers, and children do see it, and know it, and are able by the worde of God to iustifie it, and condemne you to bee aduersaries vnto the gospell in resisting it. But you think that gouernment not so needfull, and your fault but small (if it be any) in continuing your course begon. The necessitie of the thing is many wayes apparant, both in that it hath so plentiful warrant from Gods owne worde, (as the course of this booke doeth euidently declare,) and also in that the gospell can take no roote, nor haue any free passage, for want of it: and the greatnes of your fault appeareth by this, that in so doing, you are the cause, of all the ignorance, Atheisme, schismes, treasons, poperie and vngodlines, that is to be founde in this land, which we challenge to prooue to your faces, if we may indifferently be heard, and whereof in the meane while we will giue you a taste: for the first it is cleere, that you are the causers of that damnable ignoraunce, wherein the people are so generally wrapped, for that you haue from time to time stopped the streams of knowledge, in those places where the Lord in mercie bestowed the same, and in stead of able and painefull ministers, haue pestered the Churche, eyther with presumptuous proude persons, that are esteemed learned and take no paines to bring the people vnto the knowledge of Iesus Christe, or (which is the greatest nomber) such ignorant asses, and filthy swine, as are not worthy to liue in a well ordered common-wealth: and that you are the cause of all atheisme, it is plaine, for one may (as in deede many doe) professe it, and you saye nothing to him for it. If the most filthy liuer will fawne vpon you, and bribe your seruants, you will not onely fauor him, but assiste him against any godly minister or other: but if any that feare God, refuse to come vnder the leaste of your popish ceremonies, he shallbe molested, till his pursse be empty, or else by your tyrannous dealing, hee haue made shipwrack of a good conscience. And are not you the cause of all schismes, that make a hotchpot of true religion and poperye, and so giue some an occasion to fal into this course, and others into that? And it is as cleare, that you are so farre the cause of all treasons, as without you they had not bin: for if euery Church had had hir gouernment according to Christs institution; our yong gentlemen, and studentes, had not bene (for want of teaching and carefull ouersight) made a prey vnto the seducers; and consequently to those practises, which haue broght the bodies of so manie vnto Tyborne, and their soules into hell; and who but you be the cause of poperye, whilest you vse them so well, let them doe what they list, yea, and keepe them in office and authoritie vnder you, yea (whiche more is) giue them such offices as none that is not popish can execute: I speake not of the ignorance which by your means raigneth euery wher, which (as they contes) is the mother of their deuotion, and you are the wretched fathers of that filthye mother, whereby you muste needes bee grandfathers (at the least) to al kinde of popery. And who can (without blushing) denie you to be the cause of al vngodlines, seeing your gouernment is that which giueth leaue to a man to be any thing, sauing a sound Christian. For certainly it *Omnia cum* is more free in these dayes, to be a papist, *liceant, non licet esse* anabaptist, of the family of loue, yea anye moste *bonum.* wicked one whatsoeuer, then that which we should be, and I could liue these twentie years, any such in England (yea in a Byshopps house it may be) and neuer be much molested for it; so true is that which you are charged with, in a *Dialogue* lately come forth against you, and since burned by you, that you care for nothinge but the maintenaunce of your dignities, be it to the damnation of your owne soules, and infinit millions mo: Enter therefore nowe at the last, into the serious consideration of these things: remember that one day, you must be presented before the tribunall seat of Iesus Christ, to be arraigned for all the soules that haue gone to hell (seeing you will needes be the rulers of the Church) since the gospel first appeared in this land, then shall you not bee excused with this; the Queene and Councell wil haue it so: nor with

that; our state cannot beare it. For it shalbe sayde vnto
you, why do you not infourme them better of my will, why
taught you them not to worship with trembling and feare,
and to kisse the sonne least he bee angry; why did you not
tell them, that all states must be ruled by my worde, and not
my word by them and their pollicies. When these things
shalbe laid to your charge, your consciences shal aunswere;
that if you had done so, you should haue lost your dignityes,
whiche you loued and sought for especially: then shall you
wishe, that the mountains would fall vpon you, and the hills
couer you from the presence of the lambe, and from the
presence of him that sitteth vppon the throne. And I am
perswaded, that you are in league with hell, and haue made
a couenaunt with death; yea, you doe perswade your selues,
that there is no God, neyther shall there be any such day of
account; or it were vnpossible, that you should giue your
eyes anye sleepe, or take anye rest in your bedds, vntill you
had vnto the Lord by repentance, and the Church by confession, vnburdned oour souls of these hellishe wayes, wherein
you haue so long walked. Repent, repent, be not ashamed
to amend, though others haue founde you out the way, iudge
your selues whyle you haue time, least you be made fyre-
brandes of hell beyond all time. Let our challenges that wee
haue made in the name of the Lord, be hearkened vnto; Let
vs bee disputed with before indifferent iudges, let the holy
word of God bee the touch-stone to trye our disputations by,
and then shall it easily appeare, who hath the Lord on his
side, and who not. The trueth wil preuaile in spite of your
teeth, and al other aduersaries vnto it, (for God disdaineth
to be crossed, by dust and ashes.) Therefore be not obstinate
so long, as vntill you be found fighters with God; but preuent
his wrath, lest it breake foorth against you like fyre that none
can quench, because of the wickednes of your inuentions.
Venture your byshopprickes vpon a disputation, and wee will
venture our liues, take the challenge if you dare: if the truth
be on your side, you may hereby, be restored to your dignities,

and be no more troubled by vs : but if the trueth be against you, what shal it profit you to win the whole world, and afterward loose your own souls. If you refuse still our offer, then must you needes be guiltie eyther of this, that you know your cause will not abide the tryal, or of this, that you wil take no pains to confute vs that keep such a sturre in the Church : do not think that because you haue humane authority on your side, therefore you are safe, for he whose authoritie is on our side, is the greatest, to whose voice all the deuils in hell shall stoup ; much more the sillie arme of sinfull fleshe. We haue sought to aduaunce this cause of God, by humble suit to the parliamente, by supplication to your Conuocation house, by writing in defence of it, and by challenging to dispute for it, seeing none of these means vsed by vs haue preuailed ; If it come in by that meanes, which wil make all your heartes to ake, blame your selues; for it must preuail, maugre the mallice of all that stande against it, or such a iudgement must ouertake this lande, as shall cause the eares that heare thereof to tingle, and make vs be a by-word to all that pas by vs. The Lord open your eyes, that you may see the confusions whereof you are the cause, and giue you true repentance, or confounde you in all your purposes, that bee against him and the regiment of his sonne Iesus Christ. The same Lord, for the loue he beareth to his poore people ; open the eyes of her Maiestie, and the Honorable Councellers, that they may
see your godlesse practises, and in pitie to Gods people,
rid vs from you, and turne awaye his iudgementes,
which the reiecting of his holy yoke hath deserued, not punnishing them that mourne
for the desolation of Sion, with those
that spoile and make hauock of
the Lords inheritaunce.
Amen.

TO THE READER.

INfinite and vnspeakeable (Christian Reader) are the miseries from whiche Iesus Christe our Sauiour hath freed vs, and the benefites and blessings, wherewith in this life he beginneth, and for euer will continue to adorne vs. The consideration whereof (if our vnthankfulnes vnto his Maiesty, were any way proporcionable, to that which we endeuour vnto towards men) shoulde make vs continually to deuise, and all the daies of our life to studie howe wee might shew our selues (at least in some sort) carefull to glorifie his blessed name, aboue all thinges that we desire, by how muche as his loue towardes vs, excelleth whatsoeuer can else (according to our wish) befall vnto vs : but if we do with equall ballance (on the other side) looke into the course of mans life, howe well this dutie is performed; we shal see, that men declare themselues rather bent to spit in his face, and to defie him, then any way to honour him as their head and Soueraigne: for (to saye nothing of the prophane life, and the godlesse couersation, wherewith the generall number, that professeth Iesus Christ, is wholy defiled) wee see that many nations, people and languages are very willing to receiue Iesus Christe as their priest to sacrifice for their sinnes, but that he should become their king, to prescribe lawes vnto them, whereby they may bee ruled, is of all other things the most vnsauory, yea (if it be offered) the most grieuous tydinges, and vnreasonable request : wherein, albeit manye nations that haue renounced that whore of Rome, are heynously sinnefull against his glorious maiestie : yet is there none in the whole worlde so far out of square as Englande, in reteyning that popishe hierarchie, firste coyned in the midst of the mistery of iniquitie, and that filthie sinck of the Canon law, which was inuented and patched together, for the confirming and increasing of the kingdome of Antichrist : Wherein as great indignitie is offered vnto Iesus Christ, in committing his Church vnto the gouerement of the same, as can be, by meane vnderlings vnto a king; in committing his beloued spouse vnto the direction of the mistresse of the Stewes, and enforcing hir to liue after the orders of a brothelhouse. For the reformation wherof, while some haue written, and others according to their callinges, carefully stoode, how heynously it hath beene taken, howe hardly they haue bene vsed, and what shamefull reproches haue beene offered (euen vnto the course of the Gospell) for spyte that hath beene borne vnto reformation, almost by all estates and degrees, lamentable experience hath taught many of vs: but our posterity shall knowe it more particulerly, and the Church thoroughout the world shall discerne and iudge of it more euidently, when their bodies are rotten in the dust, and their soules (if they repent not) in eternall and intollerable torments; who haue reiected a request so holy, profitable and reasonable; yea, and handled the intreaters for the same so cruelly, vnchristianly and vnlawfully: but they would gladly perswade themselues (if their conscience would let them) that they haue onely executed iustice vpon vs as malefactours, and they perswade men that we desire a thing, not warranted by the worde, not heard of in the Church of God, vntill within this few years, nor tollerable in any christian common-weal whatsoeuer: The whiche monstrous slaunders, albeit they haue bene manye wayes, and by many men of most worthie gifts detected, and made knowne in those seuerall bookes that haue bene published concerning the same: yet haue I thought it necessarie (in another course) to write also of it. The course of my enterprise, is first in respect of the fauorers of the desired reformation; secondly of the aduersaries of the same, the fauourers of it, are also of two sorts; ministers of the word, and priuate persons, and both I hope, may haue profit by it. Concerning the former, when these wofull troubles that were renewed vpon vs (by that wretched subscription, that was euery where vrged) did begin to increase, I thought it meete to betake my selfe vnto that which I had read, or might any way by studie finde out, concerning the cause, and collected all into a briefe sum, and referred euery thing vnto some head; whiche beeing euer present with me, might furnish me to answere in the defence of the trueth, though it were of a sodden, by which (thorow the blessing of God) I found such profite in my seuerall troubles, that I thought it a course not altogether vnprofitable for others also, and vpon that occasion betooke my selfe vnto a more serious meditation about the matter,

and communicating the thing with diuers very worthy men;
I found encouragement and hartening on, generally by all
whom I made acquainted therwith: so that I trust (the
iudgments, yea and wishes also of others, so iumping with mine)
many ministers that loue the cause, and haue not so thorowly
studied it as were meet they should, may reape some profit
therby. Now concerning priuate men that loue the cause,
som haue great affaires in hand, and haue no leasure to read
the seuerall books of this argumente: some when they read,
are not of sufficient capacity to conceiue the force of a reason,
or to make vse of it, to enform themselues in the grounded
knowledge of the cause thereby: some (which is the generall
falt of our religious gentlemen) will take no paines to read,
some are poore and not able to buie the books which might
let them see the cause, al these (I hope) may finde helpe in
some measure hereby. Nowe concerning the aduersaries vnto
the cause, they are of two sortes also, they that know it, and
they that are ignoraunt of it. The former, if they write anye
thing against it, are contented to deal in so rouing a course
as may rather arise vnto great volumes, then soundly to saye
anye thing againste the cause: Wherein D. Whitgifte, but
especially D. Bridges, haue giuen vs an euident example: and
these with others of their iudgment (though non in these
latter days, haue written more vnlearnedly then they, of any
argument of diuinity whatsoeuer) are contented to make the
world belieue (if men will be so wilfully seduced) that our
arguments be no arguments, that they be grounded vpon false
foundations, and that we are not able to conclude our cause
in any forme of reasoning. The course that is here taken (I
trust) shall shew that they are liars: the other sort of aduersaries be they that be meerly ignorant of any thing, either for
it or against it; and perswading themselues that the sway and
shew of the worlde must needs cary the truth with it, do (like
blind bayardes) boldly venture to say any thing against it,
and think they do wel. Now of all these sorts of people, I
haue to request some thing, I hope I shall obtaine my request
(at the least) at the hands of some of them. The first sort of
fauorers (which be the ministers) I intreat, that as they ten-
der the glory of God, and honour of the cause which they
stand in; so they would diligently imploy themselues in this,
that they may be founde able to defend the same by sounde

and euident grounds out of the worde, and so muche the rather, for that the aduersaries doe greatly triumph, when they meete with one that professeth the cause, and is not able to defende it, and confute the gainsayers of it. The second sort of fauorers, be the priuate persons that loue the cause, whom I beseech to be carefull (as of all other pointes of religion) of this, that they growe in the knowledge of the word of God, whereby they may be able, vpon their owne knowledge to defend the truth, and not giue the enemie any occasion to think or say, that they be of that minde, because such and suche ministers, whom they do affect, do thinke so. Now concerning the former sort of aduersaries, to wit, they that know it, I pray them to looke into their owne hearts, and they shal finde they mislike it; eyther because it correcteth their excessiue pompe and maintenaunce, or requireth more trauaile in their ministery, then they are willing to vndergo, or at the least, controlleth that dissolutnes of behauior, wherin they willingly wallow: and if it would please god to bring them to a serious meditation of this, that it is the will of the mighty God (before whom they must be called to giue an account) whiche they doe resist, they would (I doubt not) more carefully looke about them. And lastly for them that being ignorant of the cause, speake euill of that they know not: let them (if they will bee admonished) vouchsafe to reade this little book, and wey the reasons with an vpright iudgment, which shal cause them (at the least) to suspend their sharpe censures, which so vsually appeare in their ordinary communication: and concerning vs al, let vs know (for one day we shalbe sure to feel it) that the controuersie is not about goats woolle (as the prouerbe sayth) neither light and trifling maters, which may safely be folowed or reiected (as in deed the enemies of this cause do confidently affirme) but about no les matter then this, whether Iesus Christ shalbe king or no; For if none is said to be a king, but he that ruleth by the scepter of his lawes, then the turning out of these orders which christ hath prescribed in his word, for the ruling of the Church, is to giue him the tytle, and denye him the authority belonging to the same, and so (in trueth) to make him an Idol, making him to cary a shew of that which he is not, and (with the crucifiers of him) to put a reede in his hand, in stead of his yron rod; and crowning him with thorns, in stead of the crown of greatest glory; which is the cause that so many Atheists spit in his face, and so many godles persons, do make but a iest of him: but when he commeth to shew him-selfe in his glorious maiestie; it shalbe said vnto all these sorts of aduersaries: *Those mine enemies whiche would not that I should raigne ouer them, bring hither, and slea them before me.* Luke. 19, 27. The which fearefull sentence, that we may auoide, let euerye one of vs (as may stand with our seuerall callings) carefully endeuor, to aduaunce this kingdom here, which (among other assurances giuen vs from the Lord) shalbe a testimonie vnto vs, that we shall haue part in that glory, which shalbe reuealed herafter. Now concerning the order of this booke; to direct thee (good reader) vnto thy further instruction, in the points therof. Thou hast in euery chapter, diuers proofs out of the holy word of God, which must be the things wherewith thou mayest safely informe thy conscience: then shalt thou finde (also) arguments drawn from reson rightly ruled by the same word: and lastly, (because our aduersaries charge vs, that we desire a thing not known vnto the olde writers, nor agreed vpon among the newe) thou hast here the witnes of them both in so plentifull and vniforme wise, as may plainly declare, that al godly learned men of al times, haue giuen testimony vnto the trueth of it. The most of the thinges that are here expressed, I acknowledg to be gathered out of the books that haue bene published, and are extant (purposely) concerning this argument; as may appear in the seueral points, wherein thou art sent vnto them Now, lest either thou shouldst be deceiued with a diuers impression, or think me to missealleadge the authors, I am to shew thee what books I haue followed. The 1. book of T. C. twise printed, I folow the latter; of Ecclesiast discip. I folow the latine, printed 1574, and the last booke of D. Whitgift, which containeth all the former in it. The rest (as I take it) haue bene but once printed, and therfore cary no doubt in them. If thou bee satisfied herewith, giue God the glory: and promote the cause by prayer, and all other good meanes that thy calling may affoord: and pray for vs, that we may neuer shrinke, nor be ouerthrowen by the strength of them that fight against it.

FINIS.

A DEMONSTRATION
of Discipline

Chap. I.

The diffinition of Discipline, contayneth this proposition holden by vs.

THe worde of God describeth perfectly vnto vs, that forme of gouerning the Church which is lawfull, and the officers that are to execute the same; from the which no Christian Church ought to swarue. Admonition in the præface: Ecclesiasticall Discip. fol. 5. T.C. first booke, page 26. Counterpoyson page 8. Discourse of gouernment, page. 1. &c.

The Assertion of the BB. and their adherents.

THe worde of God describeth not any exacte forme of Discipline, neyther are the offices and officers, namely, and particularly expressed in the Scriptures, but in some points left to the discretion and libertie of the Churche. VVhitgift in præface, and page. 84. aunswere to the Abstract. page 33.

THe proofe of the former is the disproofe of the latter, which is thus declared.
1 These things write I vnto thee, &c. out of whiche place I reason thus. That end which Paule respected _{1 Tim. 3. 14. 15.} in writing vnto Timothie, doth the holy ghost direct al ministers vnto for euer; for it must be kept. 1. Tim. 6. 14. But he wrote to directe him in the establishing and building of the Church. Therefore that word must direct ministers for

euer: and consequently they neither may add to, nor take from it, but gouerne it onely by the rules that be there prescribed.

2 Euery house ought to be ruled by the orders of the skilfull, wise, and careful householder onely: But the Church is the house of God, and God is such a householder: Therefore the Church ought to be ruled by the orders of God onely, which are no where to be had, but in his worde.

3 That which teacheth euery good way, teacheth also how the Church must be gouerned: But the word of God teacheth _{Prouerb 2. 9.} euery good way: pro. 2. 9. therefore it teacheth how the Church must be gouerned.

4 We cannot glorifie God, but by obedience to his word; _{1 Cor. 10. 31.} in all that we doe, we must glorifie God. 1 Cor. 10. 31. Therefore in all that we doe, there must be obedience to the word; and consequently in gouerning his Church.

5 If meate and drinke be not sanctified vnto vs, but by the _{1 Tim 4. 5.} word and prayer, then much lesse is any thing holy which is done in the gouernement of the Church besides the word: But the former is true by the testimonie of the Apostle 1. Tim. 4. 5: therefore the latter must be true also.

6 All lawfull things are of fayth. Rom. 14 23. All lawfull _{Rom. 14. 23.} things that are of fayth. haue a warrant from the word, for the word is the foundation of fayth; therefore all things lawfull, haue their warrant from the word: and consequently euery lawfull action in the gouernement of the Church.

7 Eyther hath God left a prescript forme of gouernement for the Church, vnder the newe testament: or he is lesse careful for it now, then he was vnder the lawe; for his care is in guyding it: But he is as careful now for his church as he was then: Therefore hath hee left a prescript forme to gouerne it.

8 He that was as faythfull as Moses, left as cleare instruction, _{Heb. 3. 2.} both for the buylding of faith, and gouernment of the Churche, as Moses did: But Christ was as faythfull in Gods house. Heb. 3. 2: therefore he lefte as cleare instruction for them both as Moses; but Moses gaue direction euen for euery particular, as appeareth in the buylding of the Tabernacle, and order of the priesthood: Therefore hath Christe also giuen particuler direction for the gouernment of the Church.

9 If the word of God haue described sufficient ministers and ministeries, for the buylding of the Church, and keeping it in good order, then is our assertion true: But it hath set downe sufficient for doctrine, exhortation, ouerseeing, distributing, and ordering of euery particular Churche or generall Synode: Therefore is our assertion true.

<small>Rom 12. 5. 6. 7.
1 Cor. 12 28.
Ephes.4.11.&c.
See Counterp
page 11.</small>

10 That gouernement which the Apostles taught and planted, is expressed in the word of God: But the Apostles taught and planted, pastours and teachers for instruction, elders for ouersight, and deacons to distribute, and that vniformely in euery Churche, as appeareth by their writinges and practises: Therefore a certaine forme of gouernement is expressed in the worde.

11 Euery lawfull office and action in the building of the Churche, is from heauen. Matth. 21. 25. 26. <small>Matt. 21. 25. 26</small> Euery thing that is (in the ordinarie building) from heuen, is reueled in the word: Therfore euerye lawfull office and action is reuealed in the worde.

12 If God continued (in regarde of the substance) the Church administration, as wel as the things to be administred, then is the forme of Discipline described in the word: But the former is true, as appeareth by the particulars; for priests, pastours; for teaching Leuites, or doctors of the law, Teachers; for rulers of the Synagogue, Elders; for Leuiticall lookers to the treasurie, Deacons; for the Sanedrim, the Eldershipp: therefore the forme of gouernment is prescribed in the word.

13 Euery wise king that is carefull for his subiects, setteth downe Lawes for the gouernment of the same, and will haue them tyed to no other: But Christ is such a king vnto his church: Therefore hath he prescribed Lawes vnto his Church, which none therein can alter or disobey; and consequently, the certaine forme of gouernment of the Church is described in the worde.

14 That which the ministers must teach the people to obserue, is set downe in the worde of god, for they <small>Matth. 28 20.</small> may teach nothing but that which is there, Matth. 28. 20: But they are to teache them to obserue, and be obedient vnto, the particular forme of the Churche gouernement: Therfore the particular forme is set downe in the word.

15 Euery gouernment consisteth in the gouernours, matter wherabout they are to be imployed, and maner of doing it: But in the word are described all these particulars, as it is shewed in the **9.** reason: Therfore the word prescribeth a prescript forme of gouernment.

16 The Christian religion shall finde, that out of this Scripture, rules of all doctrine haue sprong, and that from hence doeth spring, and hyther doth returne, whatsoeuer, the Ecclesiasticall Discipline doth containe.

<small>Cyprian in sermone de baptismo Christi.</small>

17 We may not giue our selues the libertie to bring in anye thing that other men bring of their will; we haue the Apostles for authours, whiche themselues brought nothing of their owne will, but the Discipline which they receiued of Christe, they deliuered faythfully to the people.

<small>Cyprian de prescrip. aduersus hæret.</small>

18 It is adulterous, it is sacriledgious, whatsoeuer is ordayned by humane furie, that the diuine disposition should be violated.

<small>Cyprian lib 1. Epist. 8.</small>

Therefore if Timothie was written vnto, that he might be directed by the worde, in disposing of the Churches; if the Lawes of God onely being the housholder, must be followed in the Churche, his House; if the word of God teache vs in euerye good way, whereof the gouernement of the Church is one; if God must be glorified in the ruling of his Church, which cannot be, but by obedience to his word; if nothing be lawfull, but that which is of fayth, warranted by the word; if God haue shewed himself as carefull for his Church vnder the Gospell, as vnder the law; if Christ was as faythfull to giue direction as Moses; if in the worde be described sufficient ministers and ministeries, to buylde vp the Churche; if that gouernement, which the Apostles taught and practized, be in the worde; if euery lawfull office and action in an ordinarie building, be from heauen, and reuealed thence by the worde; if God continued the same forme (in respect of the substance) in the time of the Gospel, that was vnder the law; if euery wise carefull king, doe set downe lawes for the direction of his subiectes; if the Apostles haue taught vs to obey that which Christ commanded; if both the gouernours matter of gouernment, and maner of doing it, be set downe in the worde; if all that pertayneth to Ecclesiasticall Discipline, spring from the scriptures; if wee may bring nothing into the Discipline of the Church, but that which the Apostles haue deliuered vs; lastly, if that be

<small>The Conclusion.</small>

adulterous and sacriligious, that is not according to the worde: then it must needes followe, that God doth describe perfectly vnto vs out of his worde, that forme of gouernment which is lawfull, and the officers that are to execute the same: from the which it is not lawful for any Christian Church to swarue. And contrariwise, that is a most vntrue assertion to saye, that the officers and offices are not particularly expressed, but left to the discretion of the Church. The reasons that they alleadge against this, are in effect none, and their obiections to these reasons, not worthy to be mentioned.

Chap. 2.

Very officer in the Church, must be placed in some calling warraunted by the worde of God, and some congregation must haue neede of such a one, before he be called to any function. Wherein are these propositions.

1 No calling is lawfull in the Churche, but that whiche is directly warraunted out of the word, vnto him that executeth it. _{The first proposition.}

The BB. and their adherentes thinke otherwise, as their practize in ordeyning Archbysh. L. Byshops, Deanes, Archdeacons, Chauncellors, officialls, &c. doth plainly declare.

2 The name and office of an Archb. is contrary to the word of God. _{The second proposition.}

3 No man may be ordeined vnto any office in the Church, vntill there be such a place void as he is fit for: *T.C.* 1. booke, page 61.

They thinke otherwise, as their making of so many ministers at once proueth, and as is holden, *VVhitgift* page 222.

1 The first is prooued thus: If Iohn was constrayned to prooue his ministerie out of the Scriptures when the Priests accused him; then is no calling lawfull, that hath not his warrant in the word, for if any be priuiledged, the extraordinarye ministers (whereof he was one) are specially excepted: But he prooued his ministery by the word, as appeareth by his aunswere vnto them, in the 23. verse. Therfore no calling is lawfull in the Church, that hath not his warrant in the word. _{Reason for the first proposition Iohn 1. 23. 25.}

2 The callings vnder the Gospell must haue as good warrant as they had vnder the law, because the light of the Gospell is (at the least) as cleare as that of the law: But there was neuer any lawfull calling vnder the lawe (excepting those that were by miraculous manner confirmed from heauen) whiche had not his directe warrant out of the worde. Therefore no calling is lawfull in the Churche, whiche is not directly warranted in the word.

3 If Corath Dathan and Abiram (though they were Le-
<small>Numb. 16.</small> uites) were punished for that they had no warrant for that which they presumed to take in hande, then is euerye lawfull calling, both in generall warranted out of the worde, and particularly layde vppon the parties from the Lorde: But the former is true, as the historie teacheth vs: Therefore must the latter needes be true also.

4 That which giueth comfort vnto a man in the time of his troubles, must haue a warraunt out of Gods worde: But euerye lawfull calling giueth comfort vnto a man in the time of his troubles: Therefore euery lawfull calling hath a warrant out of Gods word.

5 That which helpeth Gods people forward in godlines, must haue a warraunt out of Gods word: for God hath promised a blessing to his owne ordinance onely: But euery lawfull calling in the Churche, helpeth Gods people forward in godlines: Therefore euerie lawfull calling hath a warrant out of Gods word.

Therefore if Iohn did prooue his calling out of the
<small>The conclusion</small> Scriptures; if euerye calling vnder the lawe, was warraunted out of the Scriptures; if Corath, &c. were punnished for enterprising that which they had no warrant for, out of the Scriptures; if comfort in troubles commeth onely from the Scriptures; and lastly, if euery helpe to godlines is warraunted in the Scriptures; then, &c.

> They confesse all these reasons to be true, but do denie that the Archbish. L.B. &c. be distinct ministers from others. *VVhitgift* page 303. which we holde *T.C.* 2. booke page 438. and prooue it thus.

1 Those thinges that haue diuers efficient causes, are diuers: Our BB. and the ministers of the worde haue diuers efficient causes, for the one is the ordinance of God, the other the constitution of humane pollicie, as themselues doe confesse: Therefore they are distinct ministers from others.

2 A diuers forme maketh diuers things: the ministers of the word, and the L. Byshops haue diuers formes: for their ordination (euen in the Church of England) is diuers, seeing one L. B. may ordaine a minister: But there must bee three to ordaine one of them: Therefore they are distinct ministers.

3 Members of one diuision are distincte one from another: the L. BB. and ordinarie ministers bee members of one diuision: for vsually the ministers be diuided into the rulers, and them that are to be ruled: therefore they are distinct ministers.

4 The things that haue diuers effects, are diuers in themselues one from another: the L. BB. and other ministers haue diuers effects; for the one effecteth rule and gouernement, the other subiection and obedience: Therefore they are diuers and distinct ministers.

5 They that be imploied about diuers things are diuers one from another: The L. Bb. and the ordinary ministers, be imployed about diuers things, for the one is exercised in generall viewe of many congregations, and the other in the particular direction of one: Therefore they be distinct ministers.

6 That which is perpetuall, and that which may be taken away by men, are distinct one from another: The office of the minister is perpetuall, Ephes. 4.13. and the Bb. may be taken away as themselues do confesse: Therefore they are diuers, and distinct ministers.

Therefore if the ministers of the worde, and L.Bb. proceed from diuers causes; if they haue their being by diuers formes; if they be members of one diuision, which (in nature) cannot be one; if they produce diuers effectes; if they be exercized about diuers subiectes: lastly, if the one be perpetuall, and the other but for a time, then must it needes followe, that they are diuers and distinct ministers one from another. The Conclusion

The name of an Archb. and also the office that he executeth, is contrary to the vvord of God. 2. The proposition and reasons for the proofe of it.

First, the reasons that prooue it vnlawfull to giue the name vnto any man in the Churche, are these.

1 No man may haue the name giuen him, which is proper to our Sauiour Iesus Christe: But the name of Archb. is proper vnto our Sauiour Iesus Christe, as appeareth in the places quoted: Therefore no man may haue the name of Archb. giuen vnto him.

That the name of archb. may be given no man.
1. Peter. 5.4.
Hebr. 13 20.
Actes 3.15.5.31.
Hebr. 12.2.

2 If the name Pope be therefore odious, because of that Antichrist, who is intituled therwith, then must also the name of Archb. when it is ascribed vnto any mortal man: forsomuch as it is the title of a speciall member of that kingdom of Antichrist: But the former is true euen by their owne confession. *VVhitgift* page 300. Therefore must the latter be true also.

Objections for the name of Archb. and answers therevnto

But they obiect diuers things against this, for the proouing of the name Archb. to bee lawfully giuen vnto some men, which together with their answers do briefly follow.

Whitgift page 318.

1 Obiection Clemens aloweth of those names, as Polydor reporteth, lib. 4. cap. 12.

Ansvvere Polydor is but the reporter, and M. Iewell hath prooued euidently against Harding that Clemens is counterfeite, and worthy of no credite.

2 Obiection Erasmus sayth that Titus was an Archbishop.

Answere He spake as the times were wherein he liued: but that prooueth not that he helde him one in deed, no more then our naming of the Archb. of Canterburye, when we speake of him, prooueth that we like and allow his authoritie.

3 Obiection Anacletus sayth that Iames was the first Archb. of Ierusalem.

Ansvvere He is forged (as our aunswers to the papists haue shewed) but a witnes of better credit calleth him onely a bishop, Euseb. lib. 2. cap. 23. and Simon bishop after him, lib. 3. cap. 22. and Iræneus saith lib. 4. cap. 63. that the Apostles ordayned bishops euery where, making no mention of Archb.

4 Obiection The Councell of Nice Canon 6. mentioneth a Metropolitan bishop.

Ansvvere That prooueth nothing, for it was onely as much as to say, the Bish. of the chiefe Citie.

Secondly the reasons that prooue the office of the Archb. vnlawfull be these.

That the office of Archb. is vnlawfull.

1 Euery ministery that is lawful, must be of God: The office of the Archb. is not of God, for that he is not described in the worde, and themselues confesse that he is of humane pollicie: Therefore the office of the Archb. is vnlawfull.

2 That ministery whose original is vnknown, hath no warrant from Gods worde, and consequently is vnlawfull: The original of the Arch. is vnknowne as they confesse; VVhitgift page 351. Therefore it is vnlawfull.

3 That office which is needles in the church is also vnlawful to be exercised in the same: The office of the Archb. is needlesse, for the ministery is perfect without it, as the Apostle prooueth, Ephes. 4. 13. Therefore the office of an Archb. is vnlawfull.

4 If all the giftes needful for the perfecting of the Church, be appropriated vnto other ministeries, then is his ministery vnlawful: But al the needful gifts, are appropriated vnto pastors[,] doctors, elders and deacons, whereof he is none: Therefore his office is vnlawful.

5 That office is vnlawful, which none may lawfully giue: But none may lawfully bestowe the office of an Archb. because none can giue any newe giftes to adorne him withall: Therefore his office is vnlawfull.

This reason being vsed of all sounde diuines against the pope, is of the same valewe against the Archb.

6 If the office of an Archb. be lawfull, then it is eyther in respect of his excellencie aboue other men, or the place whereof he is aboue other places: But neyther of these haue euer bene, neyther hereafter can be: Therefore that office is vnlawfull.

Therefore if the office of the Archb. be not of God; if the original of it be vnknown; if in the Church it be needlesse; if all the gifts that God hath bestowed vppon his ministery be appropriated vnto those Church officers, whereof he is none; if none may lawfully bestow such an office vpon any; if it can neyther bee incident vnto any one man for his excellencie, nor his place for preheminence: then must it needs follow, that his office is vnlawfull.

The conclusion

Caluin in his Institut. booke 4. cap. 11. sect. 7. alleadgeth diuers reasons to this purpose, and Beza in his booke of diuorcements, stretcheth the same to all the inferiour officers vnder him saying: Officials, proctors, promotours, and all that swinish filth, now of long time hath wasted the Churche. So doth Peter Martyr vppon the Rom. 13. speaking against ciuill Iurisdiction in Byshops, doth by the same reasons condemne it in their substitutes.

But this being the corner stone of their building, they labour to support it with many props the most special whereof are these.

1 Obiection Cyprian sayth, lib. 1. Epist. 3. *ad Cornelium*, Neyther haue hæresies and schismes risen of anye other occasion, then of that, that the prieste of God is not obeyed, neyther one priest for the time, and one iudge for the time in the stead of Christ thought vpon, to whome if the whole brotherhood woulde be obedient according to Gods teachinge, no man woulde mooue any thing against the College of priests

<small>Obiections for the office of the Archb: and answers thervnto.</small>

Ansvvere This place is alleaged for the pope and the answere that M. Iewel and others make to it, serueth our turne: onely let this be noted, that Cyprian speaketh of the people at Rome, that had receiued another bishop (besides Cornelius) who was an hæretike; for all the course of his writings, condemneth this superioritie. It is expounded by M. Iewel, booke 1. sect. 4. diuision 5, of euery bishop: and so is it by M. Nowell against Dorman, booke 1. page 25. and also by M. Foxe, tom. 1. fol. 93. See T.C. in his 1. reply page 98. &c.

2 Obiection The authority of the Archb. preserueth vnitie.

Ansvvere Cyprian lib. 4. Epist. 9. sayth that vnitie is reserued by the agreement of bishopps, that is of ministers, one with another.

3 Obiection It compoundeth controuersies, that els would growe to many heades without any special remedie.

Ansvvere Cyprian lib. 1. Epist. 13. sayth that the plentifull body and company of Elders, are (as it were) the glewe of mutual concord, that if any of our companye be authour of hæresie, the rest should helpe.

4 Obiection Ierome vpon Tit. 1. sayth that in the beginning a bishop and priest (meaning a teaching Elder) were all one: but when men began to say, I am of Paule, I am of Apollo[s], &c. It was decreed that one shoulde be chosen to beare rule ouer the rest.

Ansvvere From the beginning it was not so: the sayinge of Tertull. *Contra Prax.* is fitt for this: that is true whatsouer is firste, and that is false whatsoeuer is latter: and Ierome sayth in the place alleaged, that this authority is by custome and not by any institution of God; if it had bene the best way to take away diuisions, the Apostles (in whose times the controuersies did arise) would haue taken the same order.

5 Obiection Caluine sayth that the Apostles had one among them to gouerne the rest.

Ansvvere That was not in superioritie, but for order to propound the matters, gather the voyces and such like; which is meete to be in euery wel ordered meeting: but his authority is no more ouer the rest, then the speaker in the Parliament hath ouer the other knightes and Burgesses.

6 Obiection Paule was superior to Timothy and Titus.

Ansvvere Paule and they had diuers offices, whereof the Apostles office was the chiefe, the like is to be sayd of Timothie and Titus, hauing superiority ouer the other ministers, for that they were Euangelists, a degree aboue ordinarie ministers.

Therefore if the place alleaged out of Cyprian, make nothing for Archb. if vnity be not preserued by him, but by the Byshoppes among themselues; if his autho- *The conclusion* ritie make nothing to the taking away of controuersies; if it be meerly inuented by man, and not from the beginning; if it be by custome, and not by any ordinance of God; if neyther one Apostle ouer the rest, nor any of them ouer the Euangelists, nor of the Euangelistes ouer the pastours and teachers, wil serue to prooue their authority: then must it needs follow, that it is vtterly vnlawful.

No man may be ordayned vnto any office in the Church, vntill there be such a place voyde as he is *The 3 proposi-* fit for, T.C. booke 1. page 61. *VVhitgift*, page 222. *tion and reasons for it.*

1 As was the 12. place for Matthias, so is a certaine Church, to euery Church officer: But Matthias was not ordained vnto the place of an Apostle, vntill Iudas *Act 1. 20.*

by hanging himself, had made it voyde, Act 1. 20. Therefore may none be ordained vnto any office in the Church, before the place where he may be imployed, be destitute of such a one.

2 As the Apostles did in planting of the Churches, so must it bee done in the buyldinge thereof for euer: But they ordayned neyther pastour, teacher, elder or deacon, but to some certaine Church that had neede therof: Therfore may none bee ordayned vnto any office, vntill a place be voyd that hath need of him.

3 Those thinges that bee of one beginning, continuance and ending, cannot be one, before or after another: But a minister, and the execution of his ministery in a lawfull standing be so; for they be relatiues, and haue reference one vnto the other: Therfore a minister ought not be ordained before there be a ministery whervnto he is to be allotted.

4 If non[e] ought to be called to be a shepherd, that hath no flocke of sheepe to keepe: neither any watchman, that is not allotted to som place to watch: then may none be ordayned to any office, before there be a place void for him: for ministers are in this sence tearmed shepheards and watchmen: But the former is true, as euery simple man can easily perceiue: Therefore the latter is true also.

5 To do contrary to the precepts and practize of the Apostles is vnlawfull: But to ordain any officer, without a certain place wherin he may be imployed, is contrary to the precepts and practize of the Apostles, as it appeareth, Tit. 1. 5. Act. 14. 23. Therefore to ordayne any officer of the Churche, without a certayne place wherevnto he is to be allotted, is vnlawfull.

6 It was ordayned that no Elder, Deacon, or any other Ecclesiastical officer, shoulde bee ordayned a *Apolelymenos*, that is loosely, or let at randone (but as afterward is expounded) specially in a Church of citie or towne.

<small>Councel Calcedon cap. 6. art. 15</small>

7 The ordination that is made without a title, let it be void: and in what Churche one is intituled, let him there remaine.

<small>Concil. Vrbanum test Gratuum dist. 70.</small>

8 He complaineth that ministers were ordayned, being chosen by no Churche, and so went here and there, hauing no certaine place.

<small>Ierom ad Nepotian.</small>

9 That action, which neuer is read to be practized, but by idolators is vnlawfull: To haue wandring officers, is onely found to be in idolaters, as appeareth Iudg. 17. 8. Therefore it is vnlawfull.

Therefore, if the Apostles ordayned not Mathias, vntill the place was voide; if in planting of Churches, they euer alotted officers to their proper places; if <small>The conclusion.</small> minister and ministery be of one beginning, continuance and ending; if it be with a minister, and his ministery, as with a shepheard and his flocke, that he cannot be the one, but in respect of hauing the other; if it be vnlawfull to transgresse the precepts and practize of the Apostles; if no minister in the Church, be ordained at randone; if the ordination that is without a title be voyde; if Ierome complayned of it, as a great faulte in his time; if no example be founde of it, but in Idolaters: then must it needs follow, that to ordayne any Church officer, vntill there be such a place voyd as he is fit for, is vtterly vnlawfull: and so the Bb. making of many ministers at once, and licencing of wandring preachers, is contrary to the word of God.

They will haue some thing to saye for euery action they doe, be it neuer so shamefull: that which they <small>An obiection.</small> alleage for this, is, that Paule and Barnabas did wander.

The Apostles office (and so the Euangelistes as assistants vnto them) was to prech the word, and plant <small>The answere.</small> Churches in euery part of the world: but the order that they left, is a president for us, which is that euery Church haue their proper officers, and that there be no other elsewhere to be found.

Chap. 3.

Very Church-officer, ought to execute the office committed vnto him, with all faythfull <small>Our assertion.</small> diligence, and consequently be continually resident vppon his charge, T.C. booke 1. page 65.

They deny not the proposition, but the consequent that is inferred vpon it, as appeareth by their writinges, <small>Their assertion.</small> *VVhitgift* page 246. and by their dayly practize in giuing dispensations for many benefices.

The reasons we alleadge to prooue the necessitie of perpetuall residence, and the vnlawfulnes of nonresidence be these that follow.

1 A shepheard hath a flocke to the ende to feed it continually: The minister is a shepheard, and his charge a flocke: Therefore he ought to feed it continually, and consequently to be perpetually resident, for how can he feed them from whom he is absent.

2 Where God doth place anye man, there his continuall trauaile is needfull, for God is most wise in disposing euery thing: But God placeth euery right minister ouer that people, which is his charge: Therefore his continuall trauaile is needfull there, and consequently he may not discontinue.

3 Flockes that are in danger, are (by carefull shepeards) watched night and day, Luk [e]. 2. 8. Euery congregation is a flocke in daunger, for the enemie goeth about like a roaring lyon, 1. Pet. 5. 8. and soweth tares whilest men sleepe. Math. 13. 25. Therefore euery congregation is to bee watched night and day by the minister therof, and consequently he may not be nonresident.

4 If his dutie to them requireth so muche trauayle, as may continually set him on worke, then may he not be nonresident: But it is euident (that it doth so) to all them that eyther know by the worde of God, what studie, prayer, doctrine, exhortation, &c. be required of him, or maketh anye conscience of giuing account for the souls committed to their charge: Therfore may not they be nonresident.

5 If the minister cannot apply himself fruitfully, to the capacitie of his people, vnlesse hee haue particular knowledge of their disposition, and capacitie, then is it not lawfull for him to be nonresident: for by continuall residence among them, he may knowe them and not else: But the former is true, as the small knowledge that the people get by generall teaching, doth euidently declare: Therfore is not lawful for him to be nonresident.

6 If the ministers of the Gospell, be as narrowly tyed to their charges, as the priests vnder the law, then may they not be nonresident: For they were alwayes readie in the Temple, to answere the doubts, 1. Sam. 1. 9: But it is clear that they are, because men are now as hardly trayned vnto godlines, and the enemie is as wrathfull as he was then; Therefore they may not be nonresident.

7 If the minister must be an example to his people; then must he be daily present with them, that they may beholde him: But the former is true, 1. Tim. 4. 12.   Therfore is the latter true also.

8 He whom the sheepe are to follow in and out, and must knowe by the voyce, ought to bee continually among them: A good minister of the worde is such a one, Iohn. 10. 4. Therefore he must be resident among them.

9 None can be alwayes readie to feede his flocke, that is absent from it: Euerye minister must be alwayes readie to feede his flocke, because it dependeth vpon him. 1. Pet. 5. 2. Therefore euery minister is to bee resident with his flocke.

10 Hee that must take heede to his flocke, watch ouer it, and feed it, must be resident continually with it: Euery minister must do so, Act. 20. 28.   Therefore, &c.

11 If Satan be the cause of nonresidence, then is it vtterly vnlawfull: But Satan is the cause of it, 1. thes. 2. 17. 18. Therfore it is vtterly vnlawful.

12 That which abridgeth the loue of God to his people, and comfort to the minister, that same is vnlawfull: But not to be resident doth both: Therefore it is vnlawfull.

13 That which hindreth the louing familiarity that shoulde be betwixt the minister and his people, that same is vnlawfull: But nonresidence doth so, for it maketh them strange one to another, and argueth small loue in him towards them: Therefore it is vnlawfull.

14 To be absent from them that haue interest in vs, and continuall need of vs is vnlawful, which we can see to be true in our seruants, &c: But the congregation hath an interest in the minister, and continuall neede of him: Therefore it is vnlawfull for him to bee absent from them.

15 If the priests might not dwell farre from the temple, then may not ministers be nonresident: But the former is true, as appeareth by this; that they had houses buylded close to the Temple. 1. Chron. 28. 13. Therefore the latter is true also, seeing the residence of the one is as needfull as the other, as appeareth in the **sixt** reason.

16 Let no Clarke be placed in two charges, for it is filthie merchaundize, and no man can serue two masters, and euerye one must tary in that place wherevnto he is called. _{Concil Nice canon 15.}

17 Damasus compareth them that set ouer their charges *Concil. tom. 2.* to others, to harlots that put out their children, that they may giue themselues to lust the sooner.

Theodoret lib. **18** It was ordayned that none, eyther B. or *1. cap. 19.* Elder, should go from citie to citie.

The conclusion Therefore, if a minister haue the charge of a flocke committed vnto him, to the end to feed it; if God place men, to the end to haue them there imploied; if flocks in daunger haue need of continuall watche; if the ministers dutie to his flocke requireth all that trauayle that he can performe; if he cannot be fruitfully profitable vnto them, without continuall residence; if his residence be as strictly required as theirs vnder the law; if he cannot be a patterne vnto them without he be resident; if they cannot follow him, nor know him if he be absent; if he cannot be alwayes readie to feed his flock, vnlesse he bee there; if hee cannot take heede to them, feede them, and watche ouer them, without his presence; if Satan be the authour of nonresidencie; if his absence abridge Gods loue to them, and comfort from himselfe; if absence be an hinderance to the louing familiaritie that shoulde be betwixt him and them; if they haue interest in him, and continuall neede of him; if he may no more bee absent, then the priests dwell from the Temple; if the Councel of Nice did vpon good grounds forbid it; if absence be like to the practize of an harlot; if it be not lawfull to go from place to place; then is nonresidence vnlawfull, and the practize therof contrary to the word of God.

The bellie (for which nonresidencie is defended and practized) hath no eares, therefore it is that they heare not these euident sounds; yet haue they very little to saye for it, so grosse is the error thereof; so much as hath any shewe of reason, is here set downe and answered.

1 Obiection Two parrishes may bee vnited, why then may not one haue charge of them both before, when they be two.

Ansvvere Because one shepheard may keep one flocke, though it bee great, but hee cannot keepe two, being verye little, and going in diuers pastures; againe, one man may haue so many flockes as he can lead in and out euerye Sabboth, to the exercises of religion, which is verye plaine that he cannot doe, to more then one congregation.

2 Obiection Parishes were deuided by men, as especially by Denis the Monk, Pope of Rome.

Ansvvere That is vntrue, for the Apostles deuided the Church into congregations, and placed elders ouer euery one of them, as the whol[e] course of the Acts and Epistles of the Apostles prooueth: and *VVhitgift* confesseth page 250. Therefore these mistes notwithstanding, nonresidencie must needes be vnlawfull: and certainely those that haue any sparkle of conscience, feare of God, or loue to their flockes, will neuer defend it, much lesse enter into the practize of it.

Chap. 4.

IT belongeth to the Church, to make choise of those officers which Christ would haue placed Our assertion. in the same: T.C. 2. booke 1. part[,] page 193. Ecclesiast. Discip. fol. 40. and *VVhitgift* confesseth it page 164.

They deny this, as their denying of al the arguments that bee brought for it doth prooue, *VVhitgift* page 154. 166. &c. and their practize of allowing patrons, and also being such themselues doth euidently declare.

If the former bee prooued true, then the latter must returne to Antichriste, which is thus declared.

1 That which was the continuall and constant practize of the Church in the time of the Apostles, that same Act. i. 26. is to be followed for euer, which appeareth by this, that the ordinaunces giuen from God by Paule, 1. Tim. 6. 14. are enioyned to be kept vntill Christ come to iudgement: but it was the constant, and the continuall practize of the Churches, then to haue a stroke in the choyse of their owne ecclesiasticall officers, Act. 1. and 26. where the Apostles presented two, to the peoples liking: wherof God was to be prayed vnto, to make one an Apostle. Act. 6. 3. where the Church is willed to choose their Deacons, and Act. 14, 25. where they gaue their consent in the choosing of their elders, by the stretching forth of their handes: Therefore it belongeth to the Church to choose their owne Church officers.

2 If the people had an interest in the liking of their teaching Leuites, (which were of the tribe of Numb. 8. 9. Aaron) then much more must the people now, for there was greater likelihood, that they were sent of God, then any of the common sort of men: But the former is true, as appereth

by the manner of the setting of them a side vnto that office
in the lawe: Therefore must the latter needs be true also.

3 That which pertayneth vnto all, ought to be approoued
of all the congregation: But euery ministerie in the Church,
pertayneth to all the congregation: Therefore, authority to
approoue of them, pertayneth to all the congregation.

4 That election which is most effectuall to bring the
people to obedience, is of all other the best; and to abridge
it, is vnlawfull: But election by common consent, is most
effectuall to bring the people to obedience, when they shall
see him teache or rule, whom they themselues haue chosen:
Therefore election by the Church is the best, and all other
kindes of elections vnlawfull.

5 That election which procureth greatest reuerence of the
people to their teachers and rulers is meetest, and all others
vnlawfull: But for the people to consent in the election of
their gouernours, procureth greatest reuerence, in their
hearts towards them: Therefore election by the people is
the best, and all others bee vnlawfull.

Testimonies of the ancient vvriters.

6 The minister should be chosen (the people being pre-
<small>Cyprian booke</small> sent) in the eyes of all, and should be by the
<small>1 Epist. 3.</small> common iudgement, and testimonie approoued
worthy and fit: &c. Therefore this is the lawfull vocation
by the worde of God, where those which are chosen, be
appoynted by the consent and approbation of the people.
For which also, he bringeth diuers authorities out of the
Scriptures.

<small>Ambrose</small> **7** That is truely and certainly a diuine election
<small>Epist: 82</small> of a Byshop, which is made by the whole Church.

<small>Ierome ad</small> **8** Let the people haue authority to choose their
<small>Ruffinum.</small> Clarkes and ministers.

<small>Ad Nepotia-</small> **9** They runne (speaking of the life of the
<small>num</small> Clarkes) to Byshops suffragans certaine times of
the yeare, and bringing some sum of money, they are
anoynted and ordayned, being chosen of none, and after-
<small>This is right</small> ward the Byshop without any lawfull election,
<small>our English</small>
<small>fashion.</small> is chosen in huggermuger of the canons, or
prebendaries onely, without the knowledge of the people.

<small>Nazianzen.</small> **10** In the Oration of the death of his Father,

approoueth the election by the people, at large, and confuteth them that would hinder it

11 When he appoynted Eradius to succeed him, sayth, it was the approoued right and custome, that the whole Churche should eyther choose or consent vnto their Bishop. _{Augustine.}

12 Anthimius choosing a Bishopp without the peoples consent, filled all Armenia with sedition. _{Basil. Epist. 58.}

13 Why did Peter communicate the election with the disciples? lest the matter should haue turned to a braule, and haue fallen to a contention. _{Chrisost. in act. 1}

Testimonies of generall Councells.

14 It is meete that you should haue power, both to choose, and to giue their names that are worthy to be among the cleargie, and to do all things absolutely according to the lawes and decrees of the Church, and if it happen any to dye in the Church, then those which were last taken, are to be promoted, to the honor of him that is dead, if they be worthy, and if the people choose them. _{Concil. Nicen teste Theodoret.}

15 Let the people choose, and the Byshopp approoue, and seale vp the election with them. _{The same Con. test. hist. tripart lib. 2.}

16 In an Epistle to Damasus, Ambrose &c. sayth, we haue ordayned Nectarius Bishopp of Constantinople, &c. the whole citie decreeing the same; and Flauianus was appoynted Bishop of Antioch, the whole citie appoynting him. _{Concil. constan. test. tripart. hist. lib. 9. cap. 14.}

17 When he hath bin examined in all these and found fully instructed, then let him be ordayned Bishop, by the common consent of the Clarkes and lay people. _{Concil. Carthag can. 1.}

18 Let not him be counted a prieste in the Church, whom the cleargie, and people of that citie where he is, do not choose. _{Conci.Toletan. test. dist. 51.}

19 If any Bishop after the death of his predecessor, be chosen of any, but of the Bishops of the same prouince, and of the cleargie and citizens, let another be chosen: and if it be otherwise, let the ordination be void and of none effecte. _{Concil:Gabil. canon 10.}

Testimonies out of the Emperors lawes.

20 Following the doctrine of the holy Apostles, &c. we

<small>Iustinian in cod</small> ordayne, that as oft as it shall fall out, that the ministers place shalbe voyde in any citie, that voyces be giuen of the inhabiters of that citie, that hee (of three whiche for their right fayth, holines of life, and other things, are most approoued) be chosen to the BISHOPPRICK which is most meete of them.

21 Being not ignoraunt of the holy canons: that the holy <small>Carolus Magnus dist. 63 sacrorum canonum.</small> Churche should vse her honour the more freely, we assent vnto the ecclesiasticall order, that the Bishops be chosen, by the election of the cleargie and people.

<small>Lodouicus Caroli filius.</small> **22** He decreed, that he should be Bishop of Rome, whome all the people of Rome shoulde consent to choose.

23 Lodouicke the second, commaunded by his letters, the <small>Platina in vita Andriani secundi.</small> Romanes to choose their owne Bishopp, not looking for other mens voyces, which (being straungers) coulde not so well tell what was done in the common-wealth, where they were strangers, and that it appertayned to the citizens.

<small>Idem in vita Leonis octaui.</small> **24** Let the people (sayth Otho the Emperor) choose and I will approue it.

The testimonies of the nevve writers.

25 The newe writers, as Musculus, in his Common places, in the title of Magistrats: Bullinger vpon 1. Tim. 4. Caluine Institut. booke 4. chap. 3. sect. 15. Harmon. confes. Heluet. cap. 18. and many others are on our side in this behalfe.

26 If there bee none that write against it, but the papists, and no arguments vsed against it, but those which be borrowed out of the popish writers: then doth it belong to the Church to choose their owne Church officers: But the former is true, as all that doe read them, that write of this argument do knowe, and as is manifest, by comparing Pighius, Hosius, &c. with *VVhitgift*: Therefore the latter is true also.

Therefore seeing the interest of the Church in choosing of <small>TheConclusion T. C. 2. booke 1. part. page 212.</small> their Church officers, is grounded vpon the word of God, both in commaundement, and continuall practize, both in the olde and newe Testament; seeing it is warranted by the light of common reason; seeing it is commended vnto vs, by the manifold practize of all ancient times, so long as any sinceritie remayned, not onely in the time of persecution, but also of peace; seeing it hath beene confirmed by so many generall Councels and ratified by the decrees of so many Emperors; seing it hath such a cloude of witnesses, both of ancient and latter times, of the best approoued writers; seeing none doe set themselues against it, but the papistes, or they that invade it onely with the same weapons that are fetched out of the popes Armory: it must needs follow, that it belongeth vnto the Churche to choose their Churche officers: and that the taking away of this freedom, abridgeth the libertie that Christ hath endowed his Churche withall, and bringeth her into great bondage, as Musculus truly affirmeth.

Their obiections against those things are these

1 Obiection They were then vnder the crosse, few in number, and therfore it was easily knowen who were fit.

Ansvvere The Gospell was dispersed thorow out all Asia, Affrica, and much of Europe, and they could lesse keepe together, or meete, and therefore that maketh rather for vs.

2 Obiection Wee haue many hypocrites, to whome it were daungerous to committ such waightie actions.

Ansvvere It is true, that we haue many: but it is a principle in hypocrisie, to be forwardst in such publike actions, that they may get fame thereby.

3 Obiection They had knowledge to doe it, but our people be ignorante.

Ansvvere We should also finde our people to haue knowledge, if they had teaching: but howsoeuer they choose, they cannot haue worse then ordinarily are chosen by the Bishops and patrons.

4 Obiection The Church was not then established.

Ansvvere That is vntrue, for though it wanted the helpe of Magistrates, yet the Apostles coulde and did better establish without them, then we can with the helpe of them: but if this order might be altered, it had bene fitter then, for nowe the magistraicie may compounde the differences of the Elders, which help then they lacked.

5 Obiection Drunkards, papists, &c. wil choose them

that bee like themselues, and we knowe the best disposed be alwayes the fewest.

Ansvvere Such are not of the Churche, but without, 1 Cor. 5. 12. and therefore are not to meddle in anye holy action: but if the people shoulde choose an vnmeete man, the eldershippe that gouerneth the action, is to reforme them: besides this, if Gods order had hir place, the schooles of the prophets would send them none, (for the ministers especially) to make choyse of, but meet men, that whomsoeuer they tooke, he should be found sufficient.

6 Obiection Paule commandeth 1. Tim. 5. 22 to lay his handes on no man rashly: therefore one did it.

Ansvvere Hee teacheth what to doe for his part, and though others would be rashe, yet he should not ioyne with them in it, as appeareth in the latter ende of that same verse, for that is ascribed vnto him, which also belonged vnto others, because he was the director: Caluin and Musculus expound the place so.

7 Obiection The Councell of Laodicea, decreed that the people should not elect.

Ansvvere That is, as Caluine taketh it vpon Acts 16. they might not elect alone, without the direction of some graue and good minister, which should be the manner in the elections, that (according to Gods word) we desire.

Chap. 5.

One is to be admitted vnto any publike office in the Church vntill he be thorowly examined by the eldership, both concerning his state of Christianitie, and abilitie to that place where to he is to be called, T.C. 1. book: page 38. Disci. Ecclesiast fol. 46:

They thinke one may do it, as appereth by the book of ordering, &c. *VVhitgift* page 134. and 135. and their slight passing it ouer, thorow the Archdeacons hands.

The former is prooued, and the latter disprooued thus.

1 Those that are to ordayne, must haue particular knowledge of the parties to bee ordayned, (or else they breake the rule prescribed them, 1. Tim. 5. 22.) which cannot be without

examination: But the Eldership is to ordayne euerye Churche officer, as shall appeare in the Chap[ter]. of Ordination: Therefore it belongeth to the Eldership to examine, &c.

2 The matter of greatest importance in the gouernement of the Churche, must be done by the most able gouernours of the same: The approouing or disproouing of Churche officers, is the matter of greatest importance, because the consequence of ruling well is the best, or ill the worst: and the Eldership is the Senate of most able gouernours in the Church, as shall appeare in the Chap[ter]. of Eldership: Therefore the Eldership is to examine, &c.

3 The way whereby a mans insufficiencie is best espyed and his abilitie discerned, is the fittest to examine them that are to be admitted: But by the eldership (consisting of diuers) his insufficiencie is best espyed, and his abilitie best discerned, for the common prouerbe telleth vs that many eyes do see more then one: Therefore it belongeth to the Eldership, &c.

4 They are to examine Church officers, that are least subiect to be blinded with partiallitie: But the Eldership is least subiect to partiallitie, both for that they be many, who are not so easily ouer ruled by affection or fauour, as one, as also (and that especially) for that it being the Lords owne ordinance (as shall appeare) we are to perswade our selues, that his spirit shal guyde them: Therefore it belongeth to the Eldership, &c.

5 The way that was vsed in the Apostles time in examining, is of vs to be folowed, vnles some reason out of the word to perswade the conscience, can be alleadged to the contrary, which none haue euer yet done: But many vsed in the Apostles time to examine, as appereth in chosing out one to be in the place of Iudas, Act. 1. 22. 23. and fit men for Deacons, Act. 6, 5. wherof the gouernours especially were some, for that they were to ordayn vpon knowledge, as is said in the first reason: Therefore it belongeth to the Eldership, &c.

6 They whose testimony the people may best credit, are to examine them that are to be admitted: But the people may best credite the iudgement of a company of able and sufficient men, which the Eldershipp rightly established must needes be: Therefore it belongeth to the Eldership. &c.

7 Examination belongeth vnto them which may most perswade the people of his sufficiency, and so procure gretest

reuerence vnto him in his place : But the examination by the Eldership is such : Therefore it belongeth to the Eldership, &c.

Therefore if they that are to ordain, must examine : if it *The conclusion* be a matter of gretest waight in the gouernment of the Churche, and they the most able to dispatch it ; if by them his sufficiency or insufficiency be best found out ; if they be hardliest carried away with affection or parciallitie ; if the examination was suche in the Apostles time ; if the people may (in reason) giue most credit to the examination that is by such ; if that kinde of examination perswade the people best of his sufficiencie, and procure him greatest reuerence in his place : then must it needs folow, that it pertaineth to the Eldership to examine those that are to bee admitted to any office in the Church.

There is nothing obiected against this, that hath any shew of reason in it, and therfore it were needles to set any thing downe.

Chap. 6.

Before consent be giuen to any man vnto any calling in the Churche, it must appeare (by sufficient tryall, and due examination) that he is quallified with those giftes, that the worde of God requireth in one of that place, Discipl. Ecclesiast fol. 44. T.C. 2. booke : 1. part page 368. and in many other places.

They gainsay this in two points : first in mainteining their reading ministery : secondly, in gouerning the Church, by their commissaries and officialls : which both shalbe ouerthrown, if we prooue these two propositions following, to be true by the worde of God.

The 1. Proposition. No man ought to bee receiued vnto the ministery, but such as be able to teache the trueth and conuince the gainsayers.

The 2. proposition. The Churche ought not to be gouerned by commissaries officialls and chauncellors.

1 He that may be receiued into the ministery, must be able to teache the people, whatsoeuer Christe hath commaunded, Matth. 28. 20. Onely he that is able to teache the trueth, and conuince the

The 1. proposition is thus prooued

gainsayers, can teach the people whatsoeuer Christ hath commanded: Therefore none must be receiued into the ministery, but such as be able to teach, &c.

2 That which is to be done conditionally, may not be done, if that condition be not kept: Men are to be receiued into the ministery conditionally, that is, if they bee vnreprooueable, Tit. 1. 5. 6. Therefore if they be not such as bee there discribed, they may not be receiued: and consequently, none may be receiued, but such as be able to teach. &c.

3 That which cannot be done without the manifest brech of Gods commandement, may not be done at all: To receiue any that be not able to teach, is a manifest breach of Gods commaundement. 1. Tim. 3. 1. Tit. 1. 9. Therefore no man ought to be receiued into the ministerye, that is not able to teach, &c.

4 They whome the Lorde refuseth to be his ministers, may not be receiued into the ministery: for the ministery being the Lords haruest, we may admit none to labour therein, but onely such, as he hath giuen liking of, by the rules of his worde: The Lorde refuseth to be his ministers, all those that cannot teach: Hosea 4. 6. Therefore such as are not able to teache, may not be receiued, and consequently none may be receiued, but those that be able to teach, &c.

5 He that may be admitted into the ministery, must be able to deuide the word of God aright, 2. Tim. 2. 15. Onely he that is able to teach and conuince the gainesayers, can deuide the worde of God aright: Therefore none may be admitted into the ministery, but he that is able to teach, &c.

6 He that may bee admitted into the ministery, must haue a treasury, furnished with olde thinges and newe, and must be able to bring it forth as occasion shal serue: Matth. 13. 52. Onely hee that is able to teache, &c. is such a one: Therefore onely he may be admitted &c.

7 He that can espy the enemy, and giue warning aforehand how to resist him, may be receiued into the ministery, Ezek. 33. 7. None can espy the enemie, and giue warning aforehande howe to resist him, but he that is able to teach: &c. Therefore none may be admitted into the ministery, but he that is able to teach, &c.

8 He that leadeth himselfe, and his people into hel, may not be admitted into the ministery: He that is not able to teache and conuince the gainsayer, leadeth himselfe and his people into hell. Matth. 15. 14. Therefore he that is not able to teache, &c. may not be admitted into the ministery.

<small>August. lib de past.</small> **9** Hee that preacheth not, but holdeth his peace murdereth.

<small>Gregor. 1. epist. 33.</small> **10** Hee that preacheth not, is not sent, and so he begetteth no fayth in man.

11 In that S. Paule requireth that a byshop should be wise, he barreth those, that vnder the name of simplicitye, excuse the follye of ministers.
<small>Ierome ad Oecumenium.</small>

12 We condemne all vnmeet ministers, not endued with gifts necessary for a shepherd that should feed his flocke.
<small>Confes. Heluet.</small>

Therfore, if a minister must teache vnto his people all that Christe hath commaunded; if none may be made ministers, but conditionally, if they be quallified with gifts meete for the same; if vnpreaching ministers cannot be made without the manifest breach of the commaundement of God; if they may not bee made ministers, whom the Lord refuseth to haue; if euery minister must haue a treasurie well furnished, and be able to bring forth of it when need requireth; if euery minister must haue skill to see the enemie, and to giue warning aforehand how to resist him; if vnlearned ministers draw their people to hell after them; if he that preacheth not, be a murtherer; if he be not sent, and so doe no good: if he be barred from the ministery: lastly, if he be condemned, as not to be in such a place: then must it needes followe, that none may be receiued into the ministery, but such as be able to teach the trueth, and to conuince the gainsayer.

Many are the arguments that be alleaged to this purpose, and many moe may be alleadged, (for the whole course of the scriptures tende therevnto) the testimony of all sorts of writers, is very plentifull for this purpose: yea of the very Canon law, (as the authour of the *Abstracte* hath learnedly prooued) and yet doe not our prelates rest in the same, but haue sett themselues (though in a silly manner) against it, in this sort that followeth.

1 Obiection There must bee reading in the Church, therefore a reading ministery, *VVhitgift* page 252.

Ansvvere By that reason we muste haue an officer for euery particular action, for there must be breaking of bread in the Church, and powring of water; but it followeth not, that therefore there must bee one, whose office must bee onely to breake bread, or to powre water.

2 Obiection It is better to haue readers then none, for preachers cannot be had for euerye congregation.

Ansvvere It is not better, for if they had non[e], they would seek for him that they should haue; whereas nowe, they that haue a reader onely, thinke themselues in case good inough: but if there be such want of prechers, why are so many of the most diligent and able ones turned out.

3 Obiection It is impossible to haue prechers euery where, and suche as can be had, must bee taken.

Ansvvere Sometimes you say all is well: and is it now impossible that our state shoulde obey the Lordes ordinance; this is the greatest disgrace to it that can be: and yet it followeth not, for no necessitie may warrant vs, to violate the decrees of the highest.

4 Obiection It were vncharitablenes to turne them out that be bare readers, for so they, their wiues and children might beg.

Ansvvere This is to sell mens souls for morsels of bread: shall we rather feare the begging of 3. or 4. then the damnation of 1000. but they may bee otherwayes prouided for; they neede not beg, many of them may returne to their occupations againe.

So that al these obiections notwithstanding, the conclusion remaineth sure, which is grounded vpon so many certaine and vnmooueable foundations.

The Churche ought not to be gouerned by Commissaries, and officialls, and Chauncellors.

1 They which are no Elders of the Church, haue nothing to do in the gouernement of the same, 1. Tim. 5. *The 2. proposition is thus prooued.* 17. These chauncellors, commissaries and officialls, are no Elders in the Church; whether we expound Elder for a minister, and him also, that is assistant vnto the minister in ouerseeing the Churche, or for a minister onely as they do: for none of them be ministers, and if they be, they doe not rule in this respect, that they are ministers: Therefore the Churche ought not to be gouerned by them.

2 They that must gouerne the Churche of God, must haue a warraunt for their so doing, from Iesus Christ the head of the Church: But Chauncellors, &c. haue no warraunt so to doe, from Iesus Christe the heade of the Churche: Therefore the Church ought not to be gouerned by them.

3 Those whose names offices and practize, be deriued from Antichrist, may haue nothing to do in the gouernement of the Churche: for who will suffer his wife to be gouerned by the Master of a brothelhouse: But the names, offices, and practize of Chauncellors, officialls and commissaries be such, which is playne by this, that they haue their grounde in that filthie dunghill the cannon law: Therefore they may haue nothing to do in the gouernement of the Church.

4 They that being inferiours, doe proudly tyrannize ouer their superiours, ought not to rule the Church of God, for it is meet it should be ruled by modest, humble and orderly men: But such are they (for being inferiors to the ministers of the word, as our aduersaries doe confesse, and is plaine also by the cannon lawe they crow ouer them as if they wer their slaues:) and if they doe not so, they can doe nothing: Therefore they ought not to rule the Churche of God.

5 They that liue by the faultes of men, are not fit to rule the Church of God: for they wil rather increase offences (that their gayne may increase) then orderly lessen them, as experience (also) prooueth: But suche are all Chauncellors, commissaries and officials: Therefore they ought not to rule the Church of God.

Therefore, if chauncellors, commissaries and officialls be no Elders of the Churche; if they haue no warraunt from Iesus Christe, the head of the Church; if their names, offices and practize, be deriued from Antichrist; if their office compel them (being inferiors) to tyrannize ouer their superiours; if they liue onely by the faults and offences of men: then it must needs followe, that the Churche of God ought not to be gouerned by them.

Chap. 7.

Very officer of the Church must be ordayned by the laying on of the handes of the Eldershipp, T.C. 2. booke, 1. part page 274. Discip. Ecclesiast. fol. 53.

They say it ought to be done by the bishopp alone, *VVhitgift* page 196. their dayly practize doth likewise shew it.

The former is prooued, and the latter disprooued by these reasons following.

1 As Church officers were ordayned in the Apostles time, so must they be continually, for they did lay the plot, according wherevnto the Churche must be built vnto the ende : but they were ordayned in the Apostles time by the laying on of the hands of the Eldership, Act. 6. 6. and 13. 3. Therefore the Churche officers must be ordayned by laying on of the handes of the Eldership.

2 Churche officers must bee ordayned by them that haue warrant from the worde, to assure the parties ordayned, that they are called of God : Onely the Eldership hath suche a warrant, 1. Tim. 4. 14. Therefore they ought to bee ordayned by the Eldership.

3 Many of the sentences alleadged before, out of Councells, Emperors, lawes, histories, and sound writers both olde and newe, for election not to be by one, but by diuers ; speake also of ordination, and so are forcible to this purpose.

4 Euagrius came to the office of a Bishopp vnlawfully, because onely Paulinus ordayned him, contrary to the tenure of many Cannons, which prouide, that they should not be ordayned, but by all the Bishops of the prouince, or (at the least) by three. Theodoret booke 5. cap. 23

5 When a Bishop is to be ordayned, &c. one bishop shal pronounce the blessing, and the rest of the bishops with the Elders present, shall all lay on their hands. 4. Concil. Carthag. cap. 23.

6 When a bishopp was to be ordayned, the bishops adioyning did ordayne him. Cyprian lib. 1 Epist. 4.

Therefore if Church officers were ordained in the Apostles time, not by one, but by the Eldershipp, consisting The Conclusion of many ; if they be to ordayne, that haue warrant out of the worde, to assure the parties ordayned, that they are called of God ; if ordination by one bishop be vnlawfull and contrary to many canons of Councells ; if the bishops and Elders were to laye on their hands : lastly, if the bishops adioyning were to ordayne ; then must it needes followe, that Churche officers are not to be ordained by one man, but by the laying on of the handes of the Eldership.

But they fight hard against this, because it striketh at a maine pillar of their kingdome, their chiefe grounds be these.

1 Obiection Paule and Barnabas ordayned Elders, where is no mention of any Eldership.

Ansvvere They are said to ordaine, because they being the chiefe procured it; so is Ioshua, 5. 3. saide to circumcise, which was the Leuites office, so say we, the Queene hath made a lawe, and yet not she alone maketh any.

2 Obiection Though it were so then, yet is it not so required nowe, no more then the communitie in the Apostles time.

Ansvvere There was no more communitie then (for they that thinke otherwise, are in that point Anabaptists) then is to be required now, so that instance maketh for vs.

3 Obiection Examples are no general rules to be followed.

Ansvvere Examples not contrarying anye rule, or reason of the Scripture, be to be followed, as if they were commaundementes, so that notwithstanding any thing aledged to the contrary, it remaineth vpon the former groundes most stedfast, that it belongeth to the Eldership to ordaine those Churche officers that are to be imployed in the publike seruice of God.

Chap. 8.

The ordaining of Churche officers must be done with humble prayer of the Eldership, and the congregation, Discipl. Ecclesiast. fol. 50.

Their vnreuerent beginning and proceedding therewith in a corner, is contrary to this: which is condemned by the proofe of our assertion by these reasons.

1 We are to behaue our selues in these actions, as they by whom we haue direction to doe them, haue set vs an example: But the Apostles and Elders, when they ordayned Church officers, did alwayes commende the action to God by prayer, together with those congregations, ouer which they placed them, Act. 6.6. and 14.23. Therefore the ordeyning of Churche officers must be done by humble prayer of the Eldership, and congregation.

2 The greater the action is that is in hand, the more carefull must they be that haue it in hand, to humble themselues by prayer, for the Lords assistance therein: But the ordeyning of Churche officers, is an action of most weightie importance: Therefore they that haue it in hand (which be the Eldershipp to ordayne him, and congregation to receiue him) ought to humble themselues in earnest prayer before hand.

3 They that shall haue part in the comfort or discomfort of the action, are to ioyne together in prayer vnto God for the better euent, and against the worse: But the Eldershipp and people, shall both haue part in the euent of the action: Therefore they are to ioyne together in humble prayer before hand, &c.

Chap. 9.

Churche officers must be ordayned by laying on of hands; in this they agree with vs, concerning the ceremonie it selfe, albeit neyther in the parties by whome, nor on whome it must be conferred. The proof of this ceremonie appeareth in the reasons following.

1 That which stirreth vp euerye partie, to pray with more feruencie, is profitable to be vsed: But such is this ceremonie, for it affecteth the ordeyners, when they feele him for whom they pray; and the ordeyned when he feeleth a calling and charge from God (as it were) sensiblie comming vpon him, and the congregation, when they see him seperated from the rest, by whome they shall reape muche comfort or griefe: Therefore the vse of it is very profitable.

2 That which helpeth forward the party ordained in his care, to walke with a good conscience in his calling, is profitable to be vsed: Such is the imposition of hands, for both it declareth vnto him, that he is separated of God for that purpose, and also giueth him hope, that his hand who allotted him therevnto, will alwayes assist him in the course of that calling: Therefore it is of a profitable vse.

3 That which worketh a more acknowledgment of Gods ordinance in the heartes of the people, is profitable to be vsed: Such is the laying on of handes, for it declareth vnto them, that the Lorde has placed him in that calling ouer them: Therefore it is profitable to bee vsed.

Therefore seeing the ceremonie of layinge on handes is forcible, to increase the feruencie of euery *The conclusion* partie, when they pray; seeing it assureth the calling to the partie ordayned, and giueth him an argument of good hope, for the blessing of God vppon him in the course of the same; and seeing it procureth a more perswasion in the people, that he is allotted vnto them from the Lord himselfe; it is euident that it is not a vaine and idle ceremonie (as manie do imagine) but of good and profitable vse, in al ordinations.

CHAP. 10.

THe Lord hath ordayned that there should be one byshop or pastor (at the least) president ouer euery congregation, who are of equall authoritie in their seuerall charges, and in the generall gouernement of the Churche, T.C. 1. booke, page 22. and 2. booke, 1. part, page 515.

They maintaine contrary vnto this, these two.

1 That one may haue two or mo chardges, and be absent from them, as their dispensations and practize do prooue.

2 That one minister may haue a soueraigntie, and Lordshipp ouer his fellowe ministers,

Which both being disprooued, the former assertion will remaine still sure.

Reasons against the 1. proposition.

1 One man may not haue mo charges then he is able in any measure to discharge: No man is able in anye measure, to discharge the dutie that is belonging vnto mo flocks then one, seeing he cannot preach vnto them, both in season and out of season: Therefore no man may haue mo charges then one.

2 That which maketh an open entrance to the enemie to spoile, cannot be lawfull: for one to haue mo charges then one, maketh open entrance for the enemie to spoyle, for the wolffe watcheth to deuoure, whilest the shepheard is absent: Therfore no man may haue mo charges then one.

3 That whiche hath neither precepte, nor president for it, eyther in Gods worde, or anye approoued writer, but onely from Antichriste, is vnlawfull: But such is the hauing of mo charges then one: Therefore it is vnlawfull.

4 That which declareth a minister to bee more desirous of the fleece, then to profite the flocke, that same is vnlawfull: But such is the hauing of mo charges then one, for were it not for the gaine, they would thinke one a burden as heauie as they could beare : Therefore it is vnlawfull.

5 All the reasons that bee alleadged in the third chapter, against nonresidence, are forcible to this purpose, for if he may not be nonresident, he may not haue mo charges, vnlesse he be willing to be quartered, that euery chardge may haue a piece of him.

He reckoneth them among theeues, and their action to be theeuery, condemned by that commandement. _{Hooper vpon 8. command.}

Therefore, if one man cannot in any tollerable measure discharge mo charges then one; if to haue mo maketh an open entrance to the enemie to spoyle; if it haue neyther precept, nor president for it, but onely in the kingdome of Antichrist ; if it declare the practizers to be more desirous of the fleece, then to feede the flocke ; if all the reasons that condemne nonresidency be against it ; lastly if it be playne theeuery : then must it needes followe, that one may not haue two, or mo charges. _{The conclusion}

Their obiections (such as they be) are set downe in the 3. chapter, and the answers vnto them.

The second proposition that they hold is thus.

One minister may haue a soueraigne authoritie, and Lordshipp ouer his fellowe ministers: which is thus disprooued. _{The second proposition that they holde, and reasons against it.}

1 They that haue their commission indifferently giuen them, without difference betweene one and another, are of equall authoritie, and may not be one ouer another : But such is the commission of all Gods ministers indifferently, as appeareth, Matth. 28. 19. 20. Therfore they are of equall authoritie, and may not haue any dominion one ouer another.

2 That which Christe hath directly forbidden, that may not in any case be allowed but is euer vnlawfull : But Christe hath directly forbidden, that one minister should haue dominion ouer another. Matt. 20. 25. Luk [e]. 22. 25. Therfore one minister may not haue superiority or dominion ouer another.

3 They that may not bee Lordes ouer the people of God, may much lesse be Lordes ouer the ministers, for the ministers be (in respect of the ministery) aboue the people : But a minister may not be Lordly ouer Gods people (as is testified

by him on whome they woulde father the greatest lordlines) 1.Pet.5.3. Therefore one minister may not be Lord, or haue superiority ouer another.

4 It is ordayned, and is equall and right, that euery mans cause be heard, where the fault was committed: and it is meete to handle the matter there, where they may haue both the accusers, and witnesses of the fault; which sheweth that euery minister had autoritie ouer his own flocke, and no other to meddle.

<small>Cyprian lib.1. Epist. 3.</small>

5 Bishopps, wheresoeuer they be in all the world, are equall to our bishops, or parrishe ministers and preachers; of none it can be sayde one is Lorde, another is seruaunt: whatsoeuer belongeth to the Churche, belongeth equally to all, sauing that some are of better giftes then others, howbeit such gifts cause no inequalitie or Lordship in the Church.

<small>Luther aduersus papat a Satana fundat.</small>

6 In the Apostolike Churche, the ministers of the word, were none aboue another, and were subiect to no head or president, &c.

<small>Muscul. loc. com de minist. verbi</small>

7 The honor of a bishopp, being taken from the rest of the ministers, and giuen to one, was the first step to papacie.

<small>The same vpon 2. Thes. 2.</small>

8 Christ did most seuerely forbid vnto the Apostles and their successors, primacie and dominion.

<small>Confes. Heluet. cap. 17.</small>

9 Equall power and function is giuen to all ministers of the Church, and that from the beginning, no one preferred himselfe before another, sauing onely that for order, some one did call them together, propounded the matters that were to be consulted off, and gathered the voyces.

<small>The same cap. 18.</small>

Therefore, if all ministers haue their commission indifferently giuen vnto them; if Christe haue forbidden, that one minister should haue dominion ouer another; if no minister may exercise dominion ouer Gods people; if authoritie to handle controuersies, belonged to euery seuerall congregation; if a bishopp and parish minister be all one; if in the Apostles time, no minister was aboue another; if the superioritie of one aboue another, was the first step to the papacie; lastly, if they haue equall power and function from the beginning: then must it needs followe, that no minister may haue superioritie, or exercise dominion ouer another.

<small>The conclusion.</small>

Their obiections herevnto (so many as are worthy any answere) be these.

1 Obiection Christ Matth. 20. 25. forbiddeth onely ambition, and not dominion, as Musculus expoundeth it.

Ansvvere Musculus his iudgment appeareth in the 6. and 7. reasons, the place is expounded against superioritie by Caluin, Bullinger, Zwinglius, Gualter, Hemingius, &c. But let it bee so expounded : that dominion is ambition, because it causeth a man to aspire aboue his fellow ministers.

2 Obiection The Greeke word signifieth rule with oppression, which is the thing that is forbidden.

Ansvvere That is not so, for Luk[e]. 22.25. vseth the single verbe *Keurieuem*, [κυριεύω] which signifieth simplie to rule: the sonnes of Zebedeus desired not to oppresse but to rule, which desire he reprooued.

3 Obiection Christ sayth not, no man shalbe so, but he that will be so, desiring it.

Ansvvere But Luke sayth, let the greatest be as your seruant, and therefore that is but a silly shifte.

So that their assertions beeinge ouerthrown, and their obiections answered, it remayneth, that we prooue yet more directly, that the Lorde hath ordayned, that there should be a bishop resident ouer euery congregation; which is thus prooued: *A bishop should be in euery congregation.*

1 If a bishop and minister be all one, then must there be a bishop in euery congregation, for euery man will confesse that euery congregation ought to haue a minister : But a bishopp and a minister is all one, as appeareth by this that S. Paule describeth not one quallity for the bishop, but it is also the quallitie of euery good minister; and also in that hee describeth no other minister but the bishop : Therefore there ought to be a bishop in euery congregation.

2 S. Paules bishopps and his deacons, were appoynted to one place, as appeareth both in the description of them, and the practize of the Apostles : But the deacons were in euery congregation, which appeareth Phil. 1. 1. Actes. 6. 2. that office being needfull euery where ; and in that it continued so, longer then the office of bishops, Athanasius Apol. 2. Ierome *Contra Luciferianos. &c.* Therefore there ought to be a byshop in euery congregation.

3 That which Paule enioyned to Titus, is also to be practised alwaies in the like case : But he commanded him to

ordaine Elders in euery citie, Tit. 1. 5. which are expounded
in the next verse to be bishops: Therefore there must be a
bishop in euery congregation.

<small>Ignatius ad Ph[i]ladelp.</small> **4** Euery Church should haue her Communion table, and euery Church her bishop.

5 Where there was found any worthy to be a bishopp, there
<small>Epiphan. lib. 3. tom. 1. hæres. 7</small> a bishopp was appointed, and where there was not to furnish both bishop and preaching elder (he meaneth the doctor) there the Apostles made a bishop, and left the elder.

6 If a bishop run into a slaunder, and manye bishops can-
<small>2. Concil. Carthag. tom. 1. cap. 10.</small> not suddenly be gathered; his cause shalbe heard of twelue bishops, &c.

<small>3. Concil. tom. 1 cap. 8.</small> **7** If an elder be accused, he may call sixe bishops from the places hard by.

<small>a Euseb. lib. 5. cap. 16. b Theodoret. lib. 5. cap. 4. c Socrat. 4. 26. d Quest. 16. dist. 80.</small> **8** Stories make mention of bishops of little townes, as ᵃSoticus bish. of the village Cuman: ᵇMares, bishop of a small towne called Solicha: ᶜGregory, bishop of a smal citie, called Nazianzum: ᵈThe bishop of a Castle.

9 A minister, that is to say, a bishopp, and (a little after)
<small>Ierome and Euagrium.</small> the Apostle doth plainly teach, that a minister and a bishop is all one, and (vpon Titus) a bishopp and a minister are the same: and (*ad Oceanum*) with the ancient fathers, bishopps and Elders were all one.

10 D. Barnes (in his sixt article) sayth, I will neuer
<small>Acts and Monuments. fol. 16.</small> beleeue, neyther can I euer beleeue, that one man may by the law of God, be a bishop of two or three cities, yea of a whole countrie, for that it is contrary to the doctrin of S. Paul, who writing to Titus, commandeth that he shoulde ordayne a bishop in euery towne.

11 It is pitie to see howe farre the office of a bishop is
<small>Hooper vpon the command. page 90.</small> degenerated from the originall in the Scripture; it was not so in the beginning, when bishops were at the best, as the Epistle to Titus testifieth, that willeth him, to ordaine in euery citie, &c. They know the primitiue Church had no such bishops as we haue, vntill the time of Siluester the first.

Therefore, if a bishopp and a minister be all one; if bishops
<small>The Conclusion.</small> were to be where Deacons are, who were in euery congregation; if Paule enioyned Titus to ordayne bishops

in euery city; and if euery church had her bishop a long time after the Apostles, as appeareth by the testimonies of Councels, Histories and learned writers, both olde and newe: then must it needes follow, that there ought to be a bishop in euery congregation.

CHAP. II.

For the further reuealing of the trueth, God hath ordayned, that there shoulde be in the Churche Doctors, whose office is to be employed in teaching of doctrin[e], and is an office different from that of the Pastour.

The latter part of this proposition, is the thing which especially they doe deny, which is thus prooued to be true.

1 Those whiche the Apostle (in speaking of distinct officers) doth distinguish one from another, are seuerall and distinct one from another: But the Apostle doth distinguishe the Pastoure and teacher, one from another, Rom. 12. 7. 8. and Ephes. 4. 11. euen as hee distinguisheth man and woman. Gal. 3. 28. See the Greek of them both: Therefore the office of pastour and Doctor are distinct one from another.

2 As are the gifts that adorne offices, so are the officers themselues, for the execution of the office, consisteth in the employing of the gifts: But the gifts of the pastour and Doctor are diuers, as apeareth 1. Cor. 12. 8. and by experience, for some hath an excellent gift in doctrine, and not in application, and others excel in application and exhortation, that are verye meane, in deliuering of doctrine: Therefore the office of a pastor and teacher, are distinct one from another.

3 Those that are to take a diuers course in teaching are diuers, and different in their functions, for els why should they be enioyned to take a diuers course: But the pastor is to take one course, and the Doctor another, for the one is to direct himselfe principally to exhort, and the other to attend vpon doctrine. Rom. 12. 7. 8. Therefore the office of pastour and Doctor, be distinct offices the one from the other.

4 The Ecclesiastical stories (especially speaking of the Church of Alexandria) doe vsually make a difference betwixt the bishopp and the Doctor.

5 Cathedrall Churches haue yet som shew thereof left in them, who (besides the bishopp) haue also one that readeth a Lecture in diuinitie,

6 If the distinguishing of them, make more for the buylding of the Churche, then the vniting of them; then are they to be distinguished, and not made all one: But the former is true, as appereth by this, that hardly is a people broght to a sounde knowledge of godlines, by him that instructeth in doctrine continually, and as hardly are wee stirred vp to a zealous care of our duetie, though we be exhorted continually; which both shoulde bee with lesse continuance, if one man were to performe all: Therefore they are to be esteemed distinct offices, and not parts of one office, which one is to perform.

Therfore, if the Apostle Paul distinguisheth them one *The conclusion* from another; if God do vsually bestow doctrine and exhortation vpon seuerall persons, wherein eche is found to excell, and to be no bodie in the other; if the pastor be commanded to take one course in teaching, and the Doctor another; if Ecclesiasticall stories doe vsually distinguish them; if Cathedrall Churches haue yet some steps left of the distinction; if to distinguish them, maketh more to the building of the Churche, then to vnite them: then must it needs follow, that the office of pastour, and Doctour be distinct, and different the one from the other.

CHAP. 12.

Very congregation ought to haue Elders to see into the maners of the people, and to be assistaunt vnto the ministers, in the gouernment Ecclesiastical. T.C. book 1. pag. 174. Disc. fol. 120. which they denie, *VVhitgift* p. 627. and their practize in keeping them out of the Church:

But it is prooued to be true, by these reasons following.
1 That which the Apostles established in euery congregation, ought still to continue, seeing the Churche must bee ruled by the same lawes that it was ruled by then, and needeth as great furtherance now, as it did then: But the Apostles established Elders in euery congregation, Act 14.23.

which cannot be vnderstood of preaching Elders onely; considering that the scarcitie of them was suche, as Paule was constrayned to sende Timothie and Titus to great cities, which he could hardly spare, as he often testifieth: Therefore there ought to be suche Elders, as are onely to assiste in gouernment in euery congregation.

2 Those which God hath ordayned to help forward the building of the Churche, ought to be in euerye congregation, vnlesse it may appeare that some congregation needeth not so much helpe as Christ hath appoynted: But Christ hath ordayned Elders in the Churche, for the helping forwarde of the building of the Churche. 1. Cor. 12. 28. Therefore suche Elders ought to be in euery congregation.

3 That which being wanting, the bodie can not be entire, that same must be in euery congregation: But the Elders cannot be wanting, and the Church be an entire bodie, Rom. 12. 8. which euery congregation should be, Rom. 12. 4 Therefore there ought to be such Elders in euery congregation.

4 If the word of God doe describe such Elders in the Church, then ought they to be in euery congregation, which is cleare by this, that euery congregation hath need of them, as well as any: and that euery congregation must haue all the other officers of the Churche: and that euery congregation is of equall dignitie in the bodie of Christ: But the worde of God describeth vnto vs such Elders. 1. Tim. 5. 17. Therfore they ought to be in euery congregation.

5 There is no Church that can stand without hir Eldership or councell. Ignat. ad Trall.

6 It belongeth onely to the bishopp to baptize, and the Elder and Deacon may not do it, but vpon the bishops licence. Tertul. de Baptist.

7 Neither Elder nor deacon haue right, but vpon the bishops commandement (so much as) to baptize. Ierome contra Lucif.

8 Elders fell away thorow the ambition of the teachers. Ambros. vpon 1 Tim. 5.

9 Valerius the bishopp did contrary to the custome of the Apostolicall Churches, in appoynting Augustine to preache, being but an Elder. Possidonius in vita Augustini

10 After that Arrius was conuicted of hæresie, it was decreed that elders should no more preach. Socrat. libr. 5. cap. 22.

11 The number of the Elders of euery Churche, Bucer de regno Christi book 1.

ought to be encreased, according to the multitude of the people.

12 Speaking of the Elders that were to assist the minister, *P. Martyr vpon Rom. 12.* he lamenteth that it is so fallen out of the church, that the name doth scarse remaine.

13 Certain of the people were ioyned with the pastor, in *The same vpon 1. Cor. 12.* the gouerment of the Churche, because the pastor was not able to doe all himselfe.

Caluin Institut. lib. 4. cap. 3. sect. 8. **14** There were elders that did assist the minister, in the gouernment of the Church, &c.

15 VVhitgift confesseth, that in the primitiue Church, they had in euery Church certain Seniors, pag. 638. Let it then appeare out of the word, to satisfie the conscience how it may bee left out.

16 If the platforme set down to Timothie and Titus be for all Churches, then must Elders be in all; for these Elders are there described: But it is a platforme for all Churches, and that to the ende of the world, 1. Tim. 6. 14. Therefore they ought to be in euerye congregation.

17 That which is contained in euery ministers commission to teache and practize, must be in euery congregation: but the ordination and practize of that office, is in euery ministers commission, Matth. 28. 20. or els they ordayned Elders without warrant from Christ, which none dare affirme: Therefore there must be Elders in euery congregation.

18 Wheresoeuer a bishoppe must be, there must also the Elders bee, whiche appeareth by this, that where the one is described, there is the other also: But a bishopp must be in euery congregation, as I haue prooued sufficiently in the 10. Chap. Therfore there ought to be elders in euery congregation.

19 If the Apostles laboured for vniformitie in the least things, and established in all Churches one order, then must there be Elders in euery congregation, for they were in some, as al men do confesse: But the former is true, as not onely the view of their practize declareth, but also the Apostles expresse words; Thus I teach in all Churches: Therefore the latter is true also, that in euery congregation there must be such Elders.

Therefore, if the Apostles established Elders in euery con- *The Conclusion* gregation; if Christe hath esteemed their helpe needfull to further the buylding of his Church; if without them a congregation cannot be entire; if the worde of God say that they ought to be in the Churche; if it was continued so long after the Apostles time: and be approoued by the testimonie of manie very learned, both olde and newe writers, and confessed by the greatest aduersary vnto them; if they be within the compasse of euerye ministers commission; if they are to be, wheresoeuer a bishopp must be; if the Apostles established vniformitie, euen in the meanest thinges; then must it needs followe, that there ought to be such Elders in euery congregation, as are to assiste the minister in the gouernement of the same.

They confesse it was so in the Apostles time, but seeme to say somewhat that it cannot be vnder a christian magistrate thus:

1 Obiection God hath giuen the soueraigne authoritie ouer his Church to the Christian magistrate, which these Elders would abridge.

Ansvver No more then the eldership abridged the soueraigntie of Dauid ouer Israell, for his gouernment is temporall, and theirs spirituall.

2 Obiection Gualter vpon the 1. Cor. 5. denieth it to be needfull vnder a christian magistrate.

Ansvvere Gualter denieth excommunication vnder a christian magistrate, he is as partial in this argument as *VVhitgift*.

3 Obiection The prince hath the authority that the Elders had.

Ansvvere That is no truer, then to saye the prince hath authoritie to preach the word, &c. for these be thinges, that his high authoritie must see done, but he may doe none of them himselfe.

But there be many reasons which may bee alleadged, to prooue that they are (at the least) as necessary vnder a Christian magistrate in these dayes, as they were in the time of the Apostles, as namely these: *Reasons proouing Elders as necessary vnder a christian magistrate, as in the Apostles time.*

1 The lesse able that ministers are to direct their people in the wayes of godlines, the more neede they haue of the assistaunce that God hath allowed them in his word: But ministers are now lesse able (especially vnder Christian magistrats, when men are ouertaken with ease and peace, which quench good things) then they were in the time of the Apostles: Therefore there is as great (if not greater) need of Elders now, then was in the time of the Apostles.

2 If christian magistrates be to maintayne the order that Christ hath set down for the gouernement of his Churche, then must there be Elders in it vnder a Christian magistrate, for Elders are appointed of Christ, 1. Cor. 12. 8. But Christian magistrates are to mayntaine the order that Christe hath set downe for the ruling of his Church, Isai. 49. 23. Therefore there must be Elders in the Church, vnder a christian magistrate.

3 If the rule of Christe cannot be perpetually obserued, tell the Church, vnlesse there be Elders; then must there be such vnder a christian magistrate: But the former is true, for by the Churche is there ment the Senate of ministers and Elders, as shall be prooued in the chapter of Excommunication: Therfore there must be Elders vnder a Christian magistrate.

4 If the whole gouernement of the Churche described in the Epistles to Timothie and Titus, be to bee obserued vntill the ende, then must there bee Elders vnder Christian magistrates, for they are contayned in those Epistles: But the former is true. 1. Tim. 6. 14. Therefore there must be Elders vnder a christian magistrate.

5 Where sinners are more outragious, and the best most subiect to wax cold, there is greatest neede of all the helpes that God hath ordayned to punish sinne, and to cherish well doing: But so it is vnder a christian magistrate, especially in the peace of the Church, as *VVhitgift* confesseth, page 643. Therefore there is (at the least) as great neede of Elders (seeing they are helpers appointed of God) vnder a Christian magistrate, as at any other time.

Therfore if ministers be lesse able now, then in the Apostles time; if Christian magistrates must maintaine the order prescribed by Christ; if els the rule of Christ (tel the church) cannot be still obserued; if the whole gouernment described by S. Paule, must be kept for euer; lastly if there be, (at the least) as great neede of all the helpes that can be, as euer there was: then must it needs follow, that Elders are as necessary in the Churche vnder a christian magistrate, as in the time of persecution.

Chap. 13.

THere ought to be in euery congregation certaine Deacons, endued with those quallities, whiche the worde of God describeth; whose office is onely in receiuinge the liberallitie of the Saints, and distributing it vnto the needie, T.C. 1. booke, page 190. Discip. Eccles. fol. 119.

This assertion hath two braunches, whiche both are gain saide by our aduersaries, the first whereof is this. The office of the Deacon, consisteth onely in receiuing and distributing vnto the poore, the liberallitie of the saints, which they denie, *VVhitgift* page 582. The booke of ordering, &c. that maketh it a degree of the ministery: but the proposition being prooued true, maketh their opinion and practize appeare false, which is thus: *(The 1. proposition.)*

1 That wherein Steuen and the rest were imployed, is the office of a Deacon: for the first institution of them by the Apostles, is in that example: But they were onely to attend vpon the prouision for the poore: Act. 6. 4. &c. Therefore the office of the Deacon, is only to attend vpon the distributing vnto the poore, from the liberallitie of the saints.

2 That which the Apostle maketh an ordinarye and distincte office from others in the Churche, must be attended vpon by them that are in the same office, and not be mingled with any other: But the Apostle Rom. 12. 8. maketh distributing in simplicitie, such an office as it is expounded by M. Caluin, Beza, Bucer, Martyr. &c. Therefore the Deacons office must be attended vppon, and consequently, it consisteth onely in distributing, &c.

3 That which the Apostles founde themselues insufficient for, that can no man now discharge in any tollerable measure, for they were more adorned with gifts then any be now: But they found themselues insufficient for the ministery of the worde, and distributing vnto the poore also, Act. 6. 2. Therefore no man can in any tollerable measure, discharge the office of a minister and Deacon also, and consequently, the Deacon is to attend upon distributing onely.

4 If the ministeries of the worde be perfect, without the Deacon, then may he not meddle in the same, for how may one lawfully labor, in that wherein there is no need of him: But such is the ministery of the word, where the seuerall ministers thereof are named, Ephes. 4. 11. wherein the Deacon is not contayned, as VVhitgifte confesseth, page 308. and 309. Therefore the Deacon may not meddle with the ministery of the word, and consequently must be imployed onely in distributing, &c.

5 If there bee no quallitie required in the perfect description of the deacon, which is proper to the ministery of the word, then is not he to medle with the same: But the former is true, as appeareth, 1. Tim. 3. 8. Therefore the latter is true also, and consequently, he must attend only vpon distributing, &c.

6 If it belong to the deacons office, to meddle with the ministery of the worde and Sacramentes, then is it greater, then that of the pastor, for that the doing of both, requireth greater giftes then the one: But it is not a greater, but inferiour office to the pastor, as appeareth by all those places wherein they are described, that the Deacon is described after the bishopp: Therfore his office is not to meddle with both, and consequently he must attende vpon distributing, &c.

<small>6. Concil. Constant. cap. 16.</small> **7** Deacons are ministers of tables, and not of holy things.

<small>2. Concil. vasens. Can. 4.</small> **8** In the ministers sicknes, the Deacons shal read the Homilies of the Fathers.

9 The Deacons haue need of great wisdom, although the <small>Chrisost. vpon Act. 6.</small> preaching of the worde bee not committed vnto them: and further, it is absurd that they should do both the office of preaching, and caring for the poore, considering that they be not able to do both thorowly.

10 Although (the goodes of the Church increasing) there <small>Bulling. decad 5. serm. 2.</small> were besides the Deacons, sub-deacons, and Archdeacons, yet the Deacons remained still in their charge for the poor, and were not as yet mingled with the bishopps or priestes, and with the order of them whiche taught.

<small>Bucer de reg. Christ. 14.</small> **11** The office of Deaconship, was religiously kept in the Churche, vntill it was driuen out by Antichrist.

12 This office muste of necessitie be restored as it is described. Act. 6. if England (for hee speaketh it in the behalfe of our Churche) will receiue the Discipline of Christ. The same de reg. &c. and vpon Ephes. 4.

13 Speaking of these Deacons, lamenteth that this order, is so fallen out of the Churche that the name doth scarce remaine. P. Mart. rom. 12.

14 Describing the Deacons of the Apostles time, sayth, that we after their example, ought to haue the like. Caluin Insti. lib. 4. cap. 3. sect. 9

15 The office of distributing the goodes of the church, is an ordinarie function in a church lawfully constituted; the which, sect. 30. he calleth the Deaconship. Beza. Confes. cap. 5. sect. 23.

Therefore if Steuen and the rest were imployed, onely in distributing the goodes of the Church; if the Apostle maketh the Deacons office, an ordinary and distinct office from al others in the Churche; if the Apostles were not sufficient for the ministery of the worde, and distributing; if the ministeries of the worde be perfect without the deacon; if in the description of the Deacon, no quallitie bee required, that is proper to a minister of the word; if to deale in both would make the Deacon a greater officer then the pastor; if the Councels, auncient writers, and the sounde writers of latter times, do declare that the Deacons were to be wholy imployed in the distributing of the goods of the Church; then must it needs follow, that his office is not to meddle with anye part of the ministery of the worde and sacraments, but to attend onely vpon the distributing of the liberallitie of the Churche, vnto them that stande in neede thereof. The conclusion

Their objections herevnto, be these two that follow.

1 Obiection Phillip one of the seuen deacons did preache, Actes 8. 8. therefore Deacons may preach the word.

Ansvvere Phillip was a deacon of the church at Ierusalem, while they abode together, but now he was not any more so, but an Euangelist, as he is euer tearmed after, by vertue of which office he did preach.

2 Obiection Steuen, beeing a Deacon, preached, Act. 7. 2.

Ansvver He preached not; for all that is there, was but his Apologie at the seat of iudgement, which euery man in the like case may doe, and which many of the martyrs haue done.

So that the former proposition beeing true, vpon the groundes alleadged, notwithstanding these obiections, we are to proceede to the second, which is this.

The 2. proposition. There ought to be such Deacons (as are described in the former proposition) in euery congregation, which is thus prooued.

1 That office which euerye congregation hath need of, ought to be in euery congregation : But euery congregation hath need of the Deacons office, whiche appeareth by this, that they haue poore to prouide for, (or els they must regarde the necessitie of others) and the liberallitie of others to distribute : Therefore Deacons ought to be in euery congregation.

2 That which is indefinitely appointed for the good of the Church, belongeth vnto euery congregation, as well as to any one : But suche is the appointment of the Deacons. 1. Tim. 3. 8. Therfore there must be deacons in euery congregation.

Ignat. ad Philadelph. **3** Euery Church ought to haue their office of Deaconship.

4 All the reasons (or the most of them) that are alleadged chap. 10. for a bishopp in euerye congregation, and chap. 12. for Elders in euery congregation ; are forcible herevnto.

Therefore, if there be the like neede of Deacons in one *The Conclusion.* congregation, that is in another ; if they be appointed indefinitely for the good of the Church ; if euery Church must haue their office of Deaconship ; and lastly, if there be like resons to prooue they belong to euery Church, that be for bishopps and Elders : then must it needes follow, that there ought to be Deacons in euery congregation.

Chap. 14.

There ought to be in euerye congregation, an eldership, consisting of a pastor or pastors, doctor (if there be any) and elders, whose authoritie Christ hath ordayned to be perpetual in his church, to gouerne the same onely by the rules of Gods word : T.C. 1. booke, page 175. Discip. Ecclesiast. 123. which containeth these 3. perticular propositions, defended by vs, and gainesaid by the BB. and their adherents.

1 *The Eldership ought to be in euery congregation.*

2 *The office of the Eldership is perpetuall.*

3 *The Church must be gouerned, onely by the rules of Gods vvorde.*

The first is denyed by them, *VVhitgift* page 627. and by their practize, in tying the gouernment of many Churches to the BB. sea, it is thus prooued. <small>The profe of the 1. proposition.</small>

1 Whatsoeuer Christe hath ordayned, as a meanes, to keepe men in obedience to the gospell, that same must be in euery congregation, for particuler men are in particuler congregations: But Christ hath ordayned the Eldership for that ende, as appeareth, Matth. 18. 15. &c. where Chrisost. expoundeth: *Tell the Churche:* that is sayth he, the gouernors of the Churche: Therefore the Eldershipp ought to be in euery Church.

2 Where all sortes of Elders ought to bee, there must be also the ioyning of their offices in one, for the good of that congregation ouer which they are placed: But all sorts of Elders ought to be in euery congregation, as is prooued in the 10. chap[ter] for bishopps, the 12. for Elders, &c. Therefore here must be an Eldership in euery congregation.

3 If no perticular congregation haue greater priuiledges giuen therevnto by the word of God then others haue, then must there eyther be no Eldership at all (which is false, in that Elders are prooued to be by the worde of God in the Church) or els it must be in euery congregation: But euery congregation is of like priuiledge, which appeareth by this, that it is a perfect bodie of it selfe: Therefore there must be an Eldership in euery congregation.

4 The same warrant that is in the worde of God, for to haue an Eldership in one place, is a warrant for it in all; for the word of God tyeth it, not to Churches in cities, but indefinitely to the church: But there is warraunt for it out of the worde to be some where, as appeareth by this, that the Apostles are sayd to establish it, and make mention of it: Therefore it must be in euery congregation.

Therefore, if the Eldershipp be ordayned by Christ, as a meanes to keepe men in obedience vnto the Gospell; if all sorts of Elders must be in euery Church; if euery congregation be of equall priuiledges; lastly if there bee <small>The conclusion.</small>

the lyke warraunt for it in euery Church, that is in any: then must it needs followe, that there ought to be an Eldership in euery congregation.

Whatsoeuer is obiected against this, that hath any shewe in it, is aunswered in the 12. chap[ter]. of Elders.

The 2. proposition. The office of the Eldershipp is ordayned by Christ to be perpetuall, and ordinarie for the gouernment of his church, T.C. 1. book 177 denied by them, *VVhitgift* 627. and by their practize in keeping it out: but the trueth of it appeareth by these reasons that do follow.

1 If the causes why Christe woulde haue an Eldershipp in his Churche be perpetuall, then must also the thing it selfe be perpetuall: But the causes are perpetuall, which be to gouerne the Church by the rules of his worde, and that ecclesiastically: Therefore the Eldership is perpetuall. <small>See the answere to D. Bridges page 132.</small>

2 If Christ be the author of the Eldership, and left it by the Apostles to bee established in the Church, then it is perpetuall; for his commission giuen to the Apostles, is to be obserued vnto the end of the world: But Christ is the author of it, as appereth both by his giuing of the gifts for the perticular members thereof, and the whole bodye of it; as also in that the Apostles did establish it in the Church, who went not from their commission, 1. cor. 11. 12. Therfore the Eldership is perpetuall.

3 Whatsoeuer is the commaundement of God, once deliuered by him, is neuer repealed againe, and to be acknowledged of euery spirituall man; that same is to bee receiued by the Churche of God to be perpetuall: But such is the gouernment of the Church by pastors, doctors and Elders, and so of the whole Eldership, as appereth in that they are all mentioned in the writinges of S. Paule, which are so esteemed: 1. cor. 14. 37. Therefore the gouernment of the Church by an Eldership is perpetuall.

4 That whose seuerall parts is perpetuall, and which hath perpetuall gifts giuen, for the furnishing thereof for euer; that same must needs be perpetuall: But the seuerall parts of the Eldership, as pastour, doctour and Elders, be perpetuall, as is proued in the 10. and 12. chap. Therfore the Eldership is perpetuall.

5 Whatsoeuer is grounded vpon the generall commaundements, and rules of the scriptures, that same is perpetuall: But the gouerning of the Church by the Eldership, is such, as hath partly bene prooued in election and ordination, and execution of the seuerall Churche offices, which is the greatest part of gouernement, and shall further appeare, in the censures of the Church hereafter: Therfore the gouernment of the Church by the Eldership, is perpetuall.

6 Whatsoeuer manner of gouernment hath sufficient power, and that from God, to begin, continue, and strengthen, both the gouernors of the Church in their callings, and the people in the course of obedience vnto Christe; that same gouernment is to be perpetual: But such is the gouernment by the Eldershipp, as appeareth by this, that the Apostles vsed no other: Therefore the Eldership is to be perpetuall.

7 That gouernment which the 12. Apostles, and Paule, before they consulted together, did vniformly agree in, that same must needs be of God, and consequently perpetuall, vnlesse the repealing of it doe appeare: but suche is the gouernement by the Eldership, (for all the aduersaries therevnto, confesse that it was in the Apostles time:) Therefore it is perpetuall.

8 Whatsoeuer hath the same grounds, that the preaching of the word and ministration of the sacramentes haue, the same is perpetuall: But such is the gouernment of the Eldershipp, for it is grounded vpon the commaundements of Christ, and practize of the Apostles: Therefore it is perpetuall.

9 That which hath the like groundes to bee perpetuall, that the Apostles, prophets, and Euangelists, had to be for a time, the same is perpetuall: But suche is the gouernement of the Church by an Eldershipp, which appeareth by this, that they are therefore ceased, because their gifts of im[m]ediate calling, &c. be gone, and the gifts of these, ioyntly and seuerally doe remaine: Therefore it is perpetuall.

10 Whatsoeuer is the perpetuall and ordinary remedie to cure diseases of the Church, and strengthen the health of the same, that same is perpetuall: But suche is the gouernement by the eldershipp, as appeareth by the necessitie, and profite of the seuerall offices thereof, and of this, that we are still to obserue in causes of extremities: *Tell the Church*, Matth. 18. 17. Therefore it is perpetuall.

11 That gouernement whiche was in the Church appoynted of God vnder the Law, and continued (in respect of the substance) by christ and his Apostles, and bettered (in respect of the accedents) by them, that same is perpetuall: But such is the gouernment by the Eldership, as appeareth in the **12.** reason of the 1. chap: Therefore it is perpetuall.

12 If there be any reason why this gouernment should be alterable (being once set in the Church by Christ) it is eyther in respect of the extraordinary offices ceased, or the addition of the magistrate: But not of the former, because the Churche hath neuer had any neede of extraordinary giftes, but God hath giuen them, and so will hee euer: nor of the latter, for that the magistrates office is to defende the buylding of the Church by that order which Christe hath set downe, and not to alter any thing therein: Therefore it is perpetuall.

13 Eyther this gouernement is the best and perpetuall, or els there is none, and so Christe should be thought to haue left his Church without a gouernement, which is disprooued in the **7.** and **8.** reasons in the 1. chap. for this was once established by Christ, and so was no other: But some gouernment must needes be the best and perpetuall: Therefore this is perpetuall.

<small>Confess. Heluet. Tigur. Bern. Geneua, Polonia, Hungaria, Scotland, cap. 18.</small> **14** No man may iustly forbidd (speaking of the church gouernment) to returne to the old constitution of the churche of God, and to receiue it before the custome of men.

<small>Caluin Institut. lib. 4. cap. 3. sect. 8.</small> **15** Experience teacheth this order (speaking of the church gouernment) was not for on[e] age, but necessary to all ages.

<small>P. Martyr. vpon Rom. 3.</small> **16** Though the common wealth change hir gouernement, yet the church must keepe hirs still.

17 Lamenteth, that some were found among them that are <small>Bucer de reg. Christ. 15.</small> esteemed forwardest, which would not haue the same discipline vsed now a dayes, that was in the Apostles times, obiecting the difference of times and men.

18 The Apostles haue written these lawes, (speaking of <small>M. Whitaker against Duræus</small> Discipline) not for a daye, or for the firste age, but to endure for all times to come; and therefore haue ratified them with a most earnest obtestation: 1. Tim. 6. 14. that these commandements should be kept vntill the day of the Lord.

Therefore, if the causes of once ordayning an Eldership, be perpetuall; if Christ be the author of it, and left it *The Conclusion.* in the Church by the Apostles; if it be Gods commandement, not yet repealed; if the parts of it, and gifts for it be perpetuall; if it bee grounded vppon the generall commandements and rules of the scriptures; if it haue sufficient power from God, to begin, continue and confirme a church; if it was agreed vpon by the 12. Apostles, and Paule before they met together; if it haue the same grounds with the preaching of the worde; if it haue as good grounds to be perpetuall as the Apostles, &c. to be for a time; if it be the perpetuall remedie against all the diseases of the Church; if it was vnder the law, and inriched by Christe and his Apostles vnder the Gospell; if it be neyther alterable in respecte of the extraordinarie offices ceased, nor the magistrate added to the Churche; if it be the onely gouernement, that challengeth authoritie from God; if no man may iustly forbidd it; if it be necessarye for all times; if the common wealth may chaunge hir gouernment, but not the Church; if the difference of times and men be nothing against it; lastly, if the rules that the Apostles gaue for it, be confirmed with a charge, to bee kept vntill the comming of Christ: then must it needs follow, that the gouernment of the Church by an Eldership, ought to be perpetuall.

They obiect that many inconueniences would follow vpon this gouernement, which are seuerally to be answered. *Obiections against the perpetuitie of the Eldership, and answers to the same.*

1 Obiection By this euery parrish shal follow their Seniors, and then there will be so many Elderships, so many diuers fashions, seeing one may not meddle with another.

Ansvvere The gouernement desired is vniforme for euerye Churche, and admitteth no change, no not in outward ceremonies, without a synode of the choyce men of seuerall Elderships.

2 Obiection If they being al mean men, chuse an Earle, he may not refuse, but be at their beck and commandement.

Ansvvere No man that is chosen is compelled to an office against his will, but he that despiseth to consult with others in Gods matters, because they bee poore, reprocheth God that made them, Pro. 17. 5.

3 Obiection It ouerburdeneth the parrish, to prouide for the norishment of so many church officers.

Ansvvere It is not necessary that they should prouide for any moe of them, sauing those that are exercised in the ministery of the worde, vnlesse any of the rest may need the liberallity of the Church.

4 Obiection It bringeth in a newe popedome and tyrannie into the Church.

Ansvvere It is blasphemie to tearme the gouernment of Christ so, because we refuse the tyranny of the pope, shall we therfore doe what we list, and not yeelde obedience to the scepter of Christ.

5 Obiection It is a kind of Donatisme to challenge such authoritie ouer princes.

Ansvvere And it is flattery to suffer princes to doe what they liste; this is the obiection of Gualter, who is a professed enemy to discipline.

6 Obiection It takes away princes authoritie in causes Ecclesiasticall.

Ansvvere No more then it did from Dauid in his time, nor so much as the Bb. do nowe, for the prince requireth but this, to see the church well ordered, which the Eldership aloweth and craueth.

7 Obiection It transformeth the state of the common wealth, into a meere popularitie, and will alter the gouernment thereof.

Ansvvere It neither transformeth nor altereth any thing in it, for let it be shewed what damage would come by this discipline to any magistracie, from the princes throne, to the office of the headborow.

8 Obiection It wil breed contention and partiallity in iudgement.

Ansvvere Where can be greater contention then the Bb. maintaine for their kingdome, or greater partiallitie then in them, to their kinsfolks, seruants, Sycophants, &c.

9 Obiection It wil be contemned, and so good order neglected.

Ansvvere None euer deserued more contempt, then the BB. and their officers doe, for all their pompe: but God whose ordinaunce it is, will procure sufficient awe vnto it; marke how these obiections stand together, in the **4.** it was tyrannie, and here it is too contemptible, these be contrary.

10 Obiection All alterations be dangerous.

Ansvvere Neuer (where we change from the obedience of Antichriste, to the seruice of the liuing God) was it euer dangerous to amende things amisse, by that course which is described of GOD: if it were, let the perticular of it appear, this might wel haue bin Steuen Gardiners reason for popery, in the time of king H[enry]. the eight.

The Church must be gouerned onely by the rules of Gods word, this is in effect, the proposition of the first chap[ter]. wherevnto all those reasons there alleadged may be referred; there is adouched generally, the certayne grounds of the whole discipline, against the imagined libertie left to the Church: here is affirmed the perticular direction of the Churche gouernement, by the authoritie of the Eldershipp, to proceed according to the rules of Gods reuealed will, and not by that cursed and monstrous cannon law, which is made manifest vnto vs by these reasons. *The 3. proposition.*

1 All gouernours are to execute their authoritie, by the same warrant from which they haue it: But the gouernours of the Church of God, haue their warrant to be gouernours only from the word, 1. Cor. 12. 28. Therefore they must gouerne the Church onely by the word.

2 The Churche is to be gouerned by that which the ministers may teach vnto the same, for they are taught to the ende that they may obey, and so be gouerned by the same: But the ministers may teach nothing but the worde of God, 1. Cor. 11. 23. Therefore the Church is to be gouerned onely by the word of God.

3 That which maketh the Churche obedient vnto Christ, must be the direction whereby it is to be gouerned: Onely the worde of God maketh the church obedient vnto christ. Therfore it is to be gouerned by the rules of Gods worde.

4 Euery kingdome or houshold, must be gouerned onely by the laws of the king, or orders of the housholder: The Churche is the kingdome and house of God, and his worde is the onely law that he hath giuen for the same: Therefore it must bee gouerned onely by the worde of God.

5 That which was ordayned to destroy the Churche of God, cannot be a good rule to gouerne the same by: But such is the cannon law, for it was ordained to strengthen the kingdom of Antichrist: *Abstract*. Therefore it cannot be a good rule to direct the church by, and consequently, it must be gouerned by the worde, for no other rule is offered vnto vs, but the one of these twaine.

6 That which was inuented by the dragon, that persecuteth the woman and her childe, that same cannot be good for the church, which is that woman: But such is the cannon law, for it was inuented by Antichriste, which is that dragon: Therefore it cannot bee good for the ruling of the church, and consequently, &c.

7 That which strengtheneth the power of darknes and ignorance, cannot be good to guide them, that must walke in light and knowledge: But the cannon lawe strengtheneth the power of darknes and ignorance, for it increaseth popery, as appeareth by this, that there is scarce an officer towardes it, in these dayes of knowledge, but he is a papist: Therfore it cannot be good to guide the church of God.

8 That which destroieth the church of God cannot be good to rule the same: But the cannon law destroieth it, for it crosseth euery faithfull minister in the discharge of his dutie, and euery good christian, walking in the wayes of godlines, and nippeth in the head euery good action, as experience teacheth vs: Therefore it cannot be a good rule to gouerne the churche by.

9 That which hath bred more trayterous papists in England, then the Seminaries at Rome and Rhemes, that same cannot be good to gouerne the church of God: But such is the cannon lawe, for it hath kept out discipline, nourished ignorance, and fostered superstition and popery, in all estates of people, that neuer came at those Seminaries: Therefore it cannot be a good rule to gouerne the church of God by.

10 That which nourisheth the hope of Antichriste to returne hither againe, cannot bee good to direct in the gouerment of the church: But such is the cannon lawe, for it keepeth the cages for those vncleane byrds; as Archb. and L. BB. seas, arches, cathedral churches, &c: therfore it cannot be a good rule for the direction of the Church.

11 That which all the Churches haue cast off, as vnfit for the gouernment of the Church, cannot be good for the same: But all the churches, that haue forsaken the pope (yea they that haue not receiued the discipline of Christ wholy) haue cast of[f] the cannon lawe: Therefore it cannot be good for the same.

12 Yea, we our selues mislike it, as appereth by a statute made vnder Ed[ward]. 6.

Therefore, if gouernours are to rule by the same authoritie whereby they are gouernours; if the Church must be gouerned, by that which the ministers may teache; if the worde of God onely, make the Church obedient vnto Christ; if euery kingdome must be ruled by the lawes of their king; and if the cannon lawe be ordained to destroy the Churche; if it was inuented to persecute the churche: if it strengthen the power of darknesse and ignoraunce, if it kill the Churche of God; if it breede more traiterous papistes, then the Seminaries at Rome and Rhemes; if it nowrishe the hope of Antichrists returne: lastly if all the Churches that haue forsaken the pope, haue cast it of[f] also; yea if we our selues do mislike it: then must it needs follow, that the Church ought to be gouerned, onely by that golden rule of Gods word, and not by that leaden lump of the cannon law. *The Conclusion*

Chap. 15.

The office of the Church gouernment, is meere Ecclesiastical, and therefore the gouernors of the Church may not meddle, but onely in church-matters, as for example, vocation, and abdication, deciding of controuersies, in doctrine and manners, so far as appertayneth to cons[c]ience, and the church censures, T. C. booke 1. pag[e] 206 Discipl. Eccle. 126. but they thinke that church-gouernours, may also meddle in ciuill causes: *VVhitgifte* page 749: and their practize, that take vpon them to be Councellors of state, to iudge ciuilly, as punishe with imprisonment, &c.

But this is disprooued, and so the former prooued by these reasons.

1 That which our sauiour Christ refused, because it belonged not vnto him, ruling and teaching the church, that same is not lawfull for any Ecclesiast[ical]. person to do: But christ refused to deuide the inheritance, Luke. 12. 14.

onely because he came to buylde a spirituall kingdome, for otherwise he being God, had authoritye ouer all thinges: Therefore it is not lawfull for Ecclesiasticall persons to bee iudges of ciuill causes.

2 That which was forbidden the Apostles, is vnlawfull for euery Ecclesiasticall officer, for they were the chiefe vnder christ, and had (after a sort) all offices in themselues, vntil they could plant them in others: But such dominion was forbidden them, as the kinges of the nations, and other ciuill magistrates haue, Luk[e]. 22. 28. which is, to rule ciuilly: Therefore they may not exercise any ciuill authority.

3 If necessary dueties are to be lefte, rather then our duties to the Churche shoulde not be thorowly discharged, then may not a churche officer deale in ciuill iurisdiction, which is lesse necessary vnto him: But the former is true, as appeareth by the words of Christ, to him that woulde haue buried his father, Luke. 9. 59. 60. Therefore they may not exercise any ciuil authority.

4 If he that hath an office must attend vpon it, then may he not meddle in another, for hee cannot attend them both at once: But the former is true, Rom. 12. 7. Therfore may no church officer, meddle with temporall iurisdiction.

5 As the Souldiour is in his warfare, so are church officers, in the ruling of Gods church: But the Soldior entangleth not himselfe in the things of this life, because they are of another nature to his warfare; which place Cyprian alleadgeth againste a minister, that became an executour to his friendes will: Therefore church-officers may not meddle with ciuill offices, because they are of another nature, then his calling.

6 Those thinges that in themselues are of contrary quallitie, cannot concurre in one subiect: But the gouernments of the church and common wealth be such, not onely in this, that they are the next speciall members of one generall, but also, in that the one is spirituall, and the other temporall, the one respecteth the soule, and the other the bodie. Therefore they cannot bee in one man together, and consequently, &c.

7 If the gouernment of the churche, both in euery particular mans office, and in the generall Eldership, be a matter of great waight, and the ability of man, very small in euery good action, then may not a church-officer meddle in another

calling, whereby he is made lesse able to discharge his dutie: But the former is true, as all men may see, that looke into the worde of God, what is required of such men, and knowe by the same worde, the manifolde infirmities and vntowardnes of man: Therfore the latter must needs be true also.

8 If the Apostles (who were the most able of all others) found themselues vnfitt for two offices, which were both Ecclesiasticall; then is the best church-gouernour vnfit for two, which be of more difference one from another, as be the gouernment of the church and commonwelth: But the former is true, as appeareth, Actes 6. 2. Therefore the latter must needs be true also.

9 That which we iustly reprooue in the papists, must needs (if we do like) be founde more vnlawfull and intollerable in our selues: But we iustly reprooue the papists, for hauing in their hands both the swordes, that is, the Ecclesiasticall and ciuill iurisdiction: Therefore it is more intollerable, being found in any of vs.

10 If it be lawfull for an ecclesiasticall person, to exercise the office of the ciuill magistrate, then (on the contrary) it is lawfull for the ciuill magistrate, to exercise the offices of Ecclesiasticall persons, for there is as good reason for the one, as the other: But the latter is vnlawfull; for who would like of any L[ord]. Mayor, to step into the pulpit and preach, &c. Therefore the first is vnlawfull also.

11 They may not intangle themselues with worldly offices, but attende vpon their Ecclesiasticall affaires. Canon. Apost. cap. 80.

12 None of the Clarkes or cleargie, shall receiue any charge of those whiche are vnder age, the cause of that decree, is there said to be, for that there were certain ministers, that were stuards to noble men; and in the 7. cannon, that none of them shoulde receiue any secular honors. Concil. Calced cap. 3. et 7.

13 The BB. shall onely attende vnto prayer, reading and preaching. 4. Concil. Carth. cap. 20.

14 He bringeth diuers reasons to prooue, that BB. may neither vsurpe, nor take (being offered vnto them) any ciuill office. Caluin Institut. lib. 4. cap. 11. sect. 9.

15 He sheweth how the offices are to be distinguished, and in what sort it is sayde, that the fathers delt in the things of this life, and howe the corporal Beza. confess. cap. 5. sect. 32 & 42.

punishments by the Apostles were perticular and extraordinary.

16 When both the offices meet in one man, the one hindereth the other, so that he that exerciseth the one, cannot minister the other.

P. Martyr. vpon rom. 13.

17 There is no man so wise and holy, which is able to exercize both the ciuill, and Ecclesiasticall power, and therefore he that will exercize the one, must leaue the other.

Bucer vpon. Matth. 5.

Therefore, if Christ refused to iudge in temporall causes, because it belonged not to his office; if ciuill dominion was forbidden the Apostles; if necessary duties are rather to be lefte vndone, then our diligence in the matters of the Churche shoulde bee lessened; if hee that hath an office, must attende vppon it; if wee may not be intangled with any hinderance; if the ciuill and Ecclesiasticall functions, be of contrary natures; if euery office in the Church, be more then any one can perfectly discharge; if the Apostles found themselues vnfit for two offices of like nature; if we iustly reprooue the papists for their two swordes; if a magistrate may not preach; if they may not meddle with worldly offices, nor be tutors to Orphans, but attend only vnto the ministery of the word, &c.; if they may neither vsurpe, nor take (being offered) any ciuill office; if they be to be distinguished to seuerall persons, or els one hindereth the other; lastly, if none be able to execute both, then must it needs follow, that Ecclesiasticall officers may not beare ciuill offices: and consequently the office of the Church-gouernment, is meere ecclesiasticall.

The Conclusion

Their obiections hereunto be these.

1 Obiection It countenanceth and maintayneth religion, to haue ciuill authoritie.

Objections for ciuill offices in ecclesiasticall persons.

Ansvvere It is (in deed) the papists reason for their two swordes, which M[aster]. Caluin confuteth: Institut, booke 4. cap. 11. sect. 9.

2 Obiection It is good to punishe vice by corporall punishment, that Gods word may be the better obeyed.

Ansvvere It is good to preach Gods word to men, that they may obey their prince for conscience sake; may the magistrate therefore preach? wee may not doe euerye thing that is good, but onely that which is agreeable to our callings.

3 Obiection Eli and Samuel, were both priests and Iudges.

Ansvvere They were extraordinary (for God separated those two offices in Moses, and gaue the one vnto Aaron) and so was Eli[j]ahs killing of the false prophets, and Christes whipping of the buyers and sellers out of the Temple.

4 Obiection Peter killed Ananias, therefore BB. may haue prisons.

Ansvvere It was by his worde onely, and not by anye ciuill punishment, if they can doe the like, Peters example will serue their turnes, if not, then must it be (with the former) extraordinarie.

Chap. 16.

He placing and displacing of Church-officers, appertaineth vnto the Eldership. This is prooued in the 7. chap[ter]. and their objections are there aunswered for the first part, which is the placing: but the latter part is to be cleared by some mo reasons, because the BB. do displace the best ministers at their plesure, which is proued to be a most wicked action, by these resons.

1 Those that are called vnto the ministery by the Lord from heauen, and outwardly by the meanes of men, so long as they are blameles in doctrine and conuersation, 1. Tim. 3. 10. cannot be displaced, without hainous wi[c]kednes against the manifest will of God: But suche are the ministers that the BB do daily displace, as they confesse themselues, when (euen) in their sermons they iustifie their doctrine, in saying that they differ onely in outward rites; and as their greatest enemies will saye, when they are asked of such mens liues: Therefore they cannot be displaced without great wickednes.

2 Those that are carefull to discharge the dutie of Gods ministers, both in teaching, and giuing example to their flockes, cannot be displaced without great impietie: Such are these ministers, that are daily displaced, as appereth by this, that they preache more diligently then any other, and that they followe not the course of the worlde, in adding liuing vnto liuing, but many of them (being as worthy for their giftes, as the worthiest) liue poorely, rather then they will want the comfort of a good conscience: Therefore they cannot be put to silence without great sinne.

3 To depriue Gods people of their spirituall comfort, is a grieuous and horrible wickednes: To put such to silence as are before mentioned is to depriue Gods people of their spirituall comfort: which if any man will denie, all the godly where such a one dwelleth, shall tell him hee lyeth: Therefore to displace such ministers, is a haynous and horrible wickednes.

4 That which giueth occasion to the weake to stumble and fall away from the Gospell, is a haynous and horrible sinne: But such is the displacing of those ministers, as appeareth by this, that many doubt whether that which he hath taught be true, whom the professors of the gospell do displace, and by this, that many who had made good beginnings, by the discontinuance of their teachers, doe fall away: Therefore to displace those ministers, is a haynous and horrible sinne.

5 Those whose labours God doth blesse, can not be displaced without fighting against God, and consequently great impietie: But such are these ministers that the BB. doe dayly displace, as all that loue the Gospell in euery countrye can witnes: Therfore to displace them is great impiety.

6 That action which giueth the common enemy iust cause to reioyce, and hope to get the victory, is a haynous and horrible offence: But such is the displacing of those ministers, as appeareth in euery country, where such ministers are displaced, and such enemies do dwell: Therefore to displace such, is a haynous and horrible offence.

7 That action that causeth the doers therof to be esteemed enemies to the gospell, must needes be a haynous sinne: But such is the putting of those ministers to silence, for it maketh the people that haue any loue to religion, think that they are not of God in so doing, for say they he that loueth Christ, cannot crosse the course of the Gospel as these men doe: Therefore the displacing of them is a haynous sinne.

8 That which letteth in more wickednes at once, then the diligent preaching of the worde could driue out in diuers yeeres, must needs be a haynous sinne: but suche is the displacing of these ministers: for, prophaning of the Saboth, and all disorder, commeth into a congregation the same day that such a minister, that hath long labored against it is

displaced, as experience in suche places prooueth: Therefore to displace such ministers is a haynous sinne.

9 That which interrupteth the course of the Gospell, without warraunt eyther from Gods word, or the lawes of the land, is a haynous and horrible sinne: Such is the displacing of those ministers, as is proued in al the writings on our side; and lastly, in the answere to D[octor]. Bridges: therfore to displace such ministers, is a haynous and horrible sinne.

Therefore if the ministers that bee vsually displaced, be called of God; if they discharge the dutie of good ministers, both in doctrine and life; if the displacing of them, bee to depriue Gods people of their spiritual comfort: if it giue occasion to some to doubt of the Gospel, and to fall away; if God giue a blessing vnto their labours; if the displacing of them giue the enemy matter to reioyce, and hope to ouercome; if it cause the displacers to be esteemed enemies to the Gospell; if it let in more wickednesse in one day, then preaching can throwe out in many yeeres; if it interrupt the course of the gospell, without warrant eyther from the word of God, or lawes of the land; then must it needs follow, that the displacing of those ministers is a most haynous, and horrible sinne against the Lord. *The Conclusion*

Chap. 17.

He Eldership is to admonishe euery one, by whome offence appeareth vnto them to grow in the Church: There is no question between vs, about admonition it selfe; but this they deny, that the execution of any discipline (and therefore of this poynt) belongeth vnto the Eldership; which point is prooued in the seuerall chapters going before: so that I need not saye any thing of this, sauing with (a reason or twayne) to shewe the necessitie and benefit of it in the Church of God.

1 That whiche priuate men offended, are commaunded to seeke vnto for the redresse of the offender, is a necessarie, and an ordinary way for the amendment of them that doe offend in the Church of God: But such is the admonition of those that are in authoritie, and cary the name of the Church, Matth. 18.15. see chap. 14. and the **1.** proposition of the same:

Therefore admonition in such cases by the Eldership, is a necessary and ordinary way, for their amendment that do offend.

2 That which is more auaylable to bring the offender to repentance, then priuate admonition, eyther by one, or moe, that same is verye profitable and necessarie in the Church of God: But such is the publike admonition by the gouernours of the Church, as appeareth by this, that Christe maketh it a remedy, when the other two will not preuaile, Mat. 18. 15. Therfore it is very profitable and necessary in the church of God.

3 That which maketh men more afraide to offend, then any admonition that priuate men can giue, is profitable and necessary in the church of God: But such is the Eldership, before whom men know they shalbe brought if they doe not amend: Therefore it is very profitable and necessary in the Church of God.

4 That which hath a greater promise to do good, then priuate admonition, is very necessary in the Church of God: But such is the admonition that is giuen by the Eldership, because it preuayleth when the former doth not: Therefore it is profitable in the Church of God.

5 That without which, all duties of charity cannot be exercised towards sinners, is needful to be in the Church of God: But without admonition by the Eldershipp, all duties of charitie cannot be exercised towards sinners: Therfore it is needfull to be in the Church of God.

6 That which woulde bridle the outragious sinnes of some, and keepe in the derision and mockery, that priuate admonitions do receiue, is needful to be in the Church of God: But this would admonition by the Eldershipp doe; for if men knewe that they should answere vnto the Churche for their ill demeanour, to them that rebuke them for sinning; they woulde refraine (at least for feare) from such kinde of outrage: Therefore it is needful to be in the Churche of God.

Therefore seeing publike admonition by the Eldership is to The Conclusion be sought, by those that are offended, and cannot be satisfied; seeing it is more auayleable then priuate admonition; seeing it maketh men more afraid to offend; se[e]ing it hath a greater promise; seeing without it all duties of charity, cannot be exercized towards the sinner; lastly seeing it would bridle the outragious sinnes of many; Therefore it must needs followe, that it is very profitable, and necessary to be in the Church of God.

Chap. 18.

Hose that be not reclaimed from their faultes by admonition, are by the Eldership to be suspended from the Lords supper, or being officers of the church, from the execution of their office, vntil they do eyther giue good testimony of their amendment, or iust cause to be further proceeded against. Neyther is there any controuersie betwixt them and vs, about this poynt; sauing that (as in the former) they will denie it to appertaine to the Eldership, which is prooued before.

I will therefore (for their vnderstanding that desire direction in the trueth) firste, shewe that it is a course that hath warrant in the scriptures; secondly, that it is of very profitable vse in the Church of God: the first is thus proued.

1 Whatsoeuer is enioyned, as a duetie to be done by euery christian, if he leaue it vndone, he is to be compelled by the gouernours of the Church to doe it, Luke. 14. 17. 23. But if a mans brother haue any thing against him, and he make no conscience to leaue his gifte there, and be first reconciled, Matth. 5. 24. he is to be compelled to do it: Therefore separation from the Lordes supper, is warranted by the word. *Suspention warranted by the word, being vpon such grounds as the worde setteth downe.*

2 If that commandement of Christe, Matth. 7. 6. giue not that which is holy vnto doggs, can neyther be properly vnderstood of them, that were neuer of the Churche, nor them that be excommunicated; then is it a warraunt for such separation of the vnworthy, and consequently, that separation is warranted in the word: But the former is true, as appeareth by this, that the meanest of the Iewes did knowe, that holy things belonged to neyther of them, and so the commandement had beene needlesse: Therefore suspention is warranted by the word.

3 If there be sinners that are not to be excommunicated, and yet it were offensiue to giue them the Lords supper, then is this course warranted by the word, for els should Christ haue left his Church destitute of direction, in common and vsual difficulties, which is prooued in the first chap[ter]. to be otherwise: But such sinners there are as the notorious sinner repenting; men mainly suspected of notorious transgressions, &c. Therefore suspention hath his warrant in the worde.

4 The course that God prescribed in the shadow, for corporal purifyings, must in the body (in respect of the substaunce) be obserued in the spirituall clensing of euery member of the Church: But many were separated from the publike sacrifices for a season, by reason of their corporall vncleanes, who, yet were not worthy to be excommunicated: Therefore must also some be kept from the Lordes supper for a season, who yet appeare not so haynously to haue sinned, as to deserue excommunication.

5 The church cannot without great offence, suffer one that hath fallen into some open sin, or that is vehemently suspected, to haue haynously offended, continue in the administration of any publike function: But the Churche cannot iustly displace suche a man at the first, making shew of repentance, or standing vpon his purgation: Therefore he must be separated for a time.

6 That which was commaunded vnder the law to be done to the priest, that was vncleane in body, or suspected to be a leaper; that same must much more vnder the Gospell, be done vnto the minister, or other Church officer, that hath sinned, or is suspected to haue committed a great sinne: But such a priest was to be separated from offring of sacrifices for a certaine time: Therefore much more must the like be done to a Church officer in the like case.

Therefore, if the Churche bee to compell a priuate man to The Conclusion doe his duetie; if, giue not holy things to doggs, be vnderstood of them within the church; if there be sinners that cannot with out offence be admitted to the Lords supper, and yet deserue not excommunication; if for corporall vncleannes vnder the law, they were to abstaine a certaine time; and if the Church can not without great offence, suffer him that hath committed an open sinne (though he repent) or that is vehemently suspected of a notorious sinne, continue in the execution of his office, vntil the congregation be satisfied; Lastly, if the priest that was vncleane, or suspected of leprosie, might not offer sacrifices: then is it plaine, that both the separation of some men from the Lords supper, and other from the execution of their publik[e] function for a time; is a thing warranted by the word of God.

The latter part, which is that this kind of suspention hath a profitable vse in the church of God, is thus prooued. *The vse of suspention profitable in the Church.*

1 That whiche keepeth the godly in more carefull obedience, and keepeth in the hypocrites, that they breake not out, is very profitable for the Church of God: But such is the vse of the separation from the Lordes supper, and from executing publike function in the church: Therefore it is profitable in the church of God.

2 That which remooueth (euen) the appearance of offence, from the Churche of God, is very profitable for the same: But such is the separation: Therefore it is profitable for the Church of God.

3 That which declareth vnto the world, that the Church of God is carefull to practize that which it professeth, is very profitable: But such is this separation, for it sheweth that they cannot away with vngodly life; no, not among themselues: Therefore it is profitable for the church of God.

4 That which giueth occasion to the church, to be exercised in the actions of religion, with more sound comfort, is profitable for the same: But such is this separation, for euery one shall see thereby, the vnworthy (for whose sakes, God might be angrie with them all, Iosh. 7. 11.) weeded from among them: Therefore it is profitable for the Church of God.

5 That whiche is a speciall meanes to procure the Lord (in mercie) to continue his word vnto his Church, is profitable for the same: such is this seperation; for it is a notable meanes to keepe men in obedience to that which they professe: Therfore it is profitable for the chur[c]h of God.

Therefore, if separation of the knowne, or suspected sinner, from the Lords supper, and such a church officer from the execution of his publike function, doe keepe men in obedience that be godly, and restrayneth *The Conclusion* hypocrites from outrage; if it remooue the very appearance of euil; if it let the world see, that the Churche laboureth to practize that which it doth professe; if it make euerye member of the Churche to be exercized in the actions of religion, with greater comfort; lastly, if it be a special mean to procure the Lord in mercie, to continue his word; then must it needs follow, that it is of very profitable vse vnto the Church of God.

Chap. 19.

When neyther admonition, nor suspention will serue to reclaym the offender, but that it doth appeare, that he abydeth in impenitencie, and is incorrigible, the Eldership, after mature deliberation, and commending of the party vnto the prayers of the Churche (hee yet remaining obstinate) is to proceed to excommunication: which containeth these propositions in question betwixt vs and the BB.

1 *It may not be done, but vpon great and wayghtie occasion.*
2 *It may not be done by any one man, but by the Eldership, the vvhole Church consenting therevnto.*

The former is holden by vs, T.C. 1. book, pag[e] 183. Discipl. Eccles. 130. and denied by them in their practize, that send it out (many times) for not paying of sixe pence.

But our assertion is thus prooued, and their godlesse practize disprooued.

1 That which Christ hath ordayned for the last remedie against sinne, and onely to be vsed when neyther admonition, reprehension, nor separation from the externall communion of the saynts for a time will serue; that same is not to be vsed, but vpon great extremitie: But such is excommunication, as appeareth, Math. 18. 15. Therefore it may not be vsed, but vppon most wayghtie occasion, that is in the case (onely) of extremitie, when no other meanes will serue the turne.

The proofe of the 1 proposition.

2 That whiche cutteth a man of[f] from the Church of God,

and giueth him ouer vnto Satan, as one in a desperate case, that same may not be vsed but in greatest extremitie: But such is excommunication, being vsed according as God hath left it vnto his Churche, 1. Cor. 5. 5. Therefore it may not bee vsed, but in greatest extremitie.

3 That which a man will doe in the cutting off, of his hand or his foote, that same must the Church doe, in excommunication; for it is the cutting off, of a member: But a man will trie all other wayes, and will neuer cut of[f] his hande or his foote, vntill he see it incurable, and ready to infect the other parts of his bodie: Therefore excommunication may not be vsed, but in case of greatest extremitie.

4 That which is contrary to naturall affection, and worketh that whiche a louing heart doth tremble to thinke of; that same may not be done but in greatest extremitie: But such is the excommunication, for it depriueth the party excommunicated of our loue, and throweth him into the most wretched case, that can befall vnto man in this life: Therefore it may not be done, but in cases of greatest extremity.

Therefore if excommunication be ordained of Christe, as a remedie, onely when all other helpes will not serue; if it cut the partie from Gods Churche, and giue him ouer vnto Satan; it it must be proceeded vnto, as a man doth to the cutting off of his hand or foote; lastly, if it be a worke contrary vnto the naturall affection of man, and effecteth that which a louing hart doth tremble to think vpon: then must it needs follow, that it is to be proceeded vnto, only in the cases of greatest extremitie, and after that all other meanes haue bene vsed, and do appeare not to preuaile. *The Conclusion*

The latter poynt (which is, that excommunication may not be done by one man, but by the Eldership, the whole Church consenting therevnto) is holden by vs, T.C. booke 1. page 183. Discipl. Ecclesiast: 130. &c. and denyed by them, *VVhitgift*, page 662. and their continuall practise; But our assertion is thus proued, and their opinion and practize, founde to be erroneous and vngodly. *The proofe of the 2. proposition.*

1 That which Christ commanded to be done by the Church, may not be done by one man, vnles you take my

L. Grace for the Churche as *VVhitgifte* doth, page, 662. which needeth no confutation: But Christe commanded that excommunication should be done by the church, Matth. 18. 15. Therefore it may not be done by one man.

2 That which Paule enioyned the Churche, when they were met together, to doe, may not be done by one man But he commanded them to excommunicate the incestuous person, when they were met together, 1 Cor. 5. 5. Therefore it may not be done by one man.

3 That which hath need of greatest aduice, and greatest authority, may not be done by one man: But such is the matter of excommunication, being the denouncing of that against a man, which he will most hardly beleeue, and being the wayghtiest poynt of discipline: Therefore it may not be done by one man.

4 Those must excommunicate, that are to deale in the other partes of discipline, as shall appear in the resons following, and (as I think) no man will denie: But the other partes of discipline are exercized not by one, but by the Church, as hath bene prooued: Therefore not one, but the Church is to excommunicate.

5 As it was ministred among the Iewes, so must it be in the Church for euer; which appeareth by this, that it is translated vnto vs from them (as the Greeke word *Synedrion*, being by a corrupt imitation, called *Sanedrim*, by the Rabbins, doth import) and had nothing ceremoniall in it: But it was executed among them by the Church, and not any one, Iohn 9. 22. Therefore the Church is to excommunicate, and not one man.

Cyprian lib. 3. epist. 10.   6 Sayth, he would neuer do any thing in his charge, without the counsell of his Elders, and consent of the people.

Epist. 14.   7 The elders, and other church-officers, haue as wel power to absolue, as the byshop.

Epist. 19.   8 For so much as absolution belongeth vnto all, I alone dare not do it.

9 If there be any that haue committed such a fault, that Tertul. Apol. cap. 39.   he is to be put away from the partaking of the prayers of the Church, &c. There do beare rule, certayne of the most approoued aunciente or elders of the Church, which haue obtayned this honour, not by money, but by good report.

10 It helpeth much to make the party more ashamed, that he be excommunicated by the whole Church: also in his bookes of Baptisme, against the Donatists often.

August. lib. 3. cont. epist. permen.

11 The Elders haue interest in other censures of the Church, and the Church it selfe in excommunication.

Ierom ad Demetriad. Epist. 1.

12 S. Paule accuseth the Corinthians, for that the whole Church had not excommunicated the incestuous person.

Bucer de regno Christi lib. 1. cap. 9.

13 The Elders had the gouernement in excommunication.

P. Martyr in 1. Cor. 5.

14 It is very dangerous to permit so weightie a matter to one man, and therefore that tyrannie may be auoyded, and this censure executed with greater fruite and grauitie, the order that the Apostle there vseth, is still to bee obserued.

The same vpon the same place

15 Hee sheweth that it pertayneth not to one man, that it is a wicked fact that one should take the authoritie to himselfe, that is common to others; that it openeth a way to tyrannie; taketh from the Church their right, and abrogateth the Ecclesiasticall senate, ordayned by Iesus Christ.

Caluin Institut. lib. 4. cap. 11. sect. 6.

16 The byshops, when they excommunicated of themselues alone, did it ambitiously, contrary to the decrees of godly cannons: See Bucer against Gropper, and vpon Ephes. 4. *De animi Cura*, also Zuinglius in Ecclesiast.

Chap. 12. sect. 6.

17 It is plentifully forbidden (euen) by that filthie puddle, the cannon law, and therefore it must needs be a haynous sinne, when it findeth fault with it.

See Abstract page 165.

Therefore if excommunication be to be executed (by the commaundement of Christe) of the Churche; if S. Paule enioyned it vnto the Church; if it haue need of greatest aduice and authoritie; if it belong to them that may execute the other partes of Discipline; if it was so executed among the Iewes; if to absolue, be as well in the Elders power, as the Byshops; if Cyprian durst not do it alone; if it was the action (in Tertul[l]ians time) of the most approoued Elders; if to be by the whole Churche, helpeth much to make the partie more ashamed; if the whole Churche haue interest in it; if the whole Church at Corinth was

The Conclusion

reprooued, for not doing it; if it be too weighty a matter for one man; if the executing of it by one, ouerturneth the order appoynted by Christ; bringeth in tyrannie; maintayneth ambition; and lastly, be forbidden by the cannon law it selfe. Then must it needes followe, that it belongeth not vnto one man to excommunicate, but vnto the Eldershipp, and that with the consent of the whole Church.

Their obiections hereunto in defence of their owne practize be these.

1 Obiection The right of excommunication, was in S. Paule and not in the rest.

Ansvvere He gaue onely direction in that, as in all other matters, whiche hee wrote of vnto them, but if they had not throwne out the incestuous person, he had remayned still vnexcommunicated, for all that which S. Paule had sayd vnto them.

2 Obiection Christ gaue Peter and euery Apostle power to binde, and lose in earth and in heauen, which interpreters expound by Matth. 18. 15.

Ansvvere That power was of denouncinge Gods iudgements, or pronouncing his mercie in preaching, and not of this action: they are expounded one by another, because of the ratifying of them both in heauen alike.

3 Obiection Paule did excommunicate Hymeneus and Philetus.

Ansvvere That is, beeing moderator of the action, he pronounced it, not that he did it alone; The same answere, is to be made vnto the fathers, as Ambrose, &c. who are said to excommunicate.

TheConclusion of the whole booke.

a Chap. 1.

Therefore vpon these grounds of Scriptures, Fathers, Councels, Emperours, Lawes, Histories, newe writers, and cleare light of reason. I conclude, that [a]Christ hath prescribed vnto vs an exacte, and perfect platforme of gouerning his church at all times, and in all

b Chap. 10.&11.

places; which is this [b]that there ought to be no ministers of the the word, but pastor and teachers, whiche are to be ^ccalled by the people, and ordained by the Eldership, are of ^dequall authoritie in their seuerall congregations, muste ^fwith all faythfull diligence imploye themselues, in the ministery of the worde and sacramentes, ^gthat there are to be in euery congregation certaine elders, whose office is to ouersee the behauiour of the people, and assist their pastour, in the gouerment of the church; ^halso Deacons, who are to be imployed onely in receiuing, and bestowing the liberallity and goods of the church to the reliefe of the poore, and other necessary vses: ⁱLastly, that there must be in euery congregation an eldershipp of pastour, teacher (if they can haue any) and elders, who are in common, to see that the church be well gouerned, not onely in maintayning the profession and practize of the worde in generall, ^kbut also in admonishing, reprehending, or ^lseperating from the Lords supper, them that walke offensiuely, and ^mlastly in excommunicating them, that bye no other meanes can be reclaimed. So that all and euery gouernement, contrary or besides this, whether in part or in whol[e], swarueth from that order, which Christ hath set downe in his word, and therefore is vnlawfull.

c Chap. 4.
d Chap. 7.
e Chap. 10.
f Chap. 10.
g Chap. 21.
h Chap. 13.
i Chap. 14.
k Chap. 17
l Chap. 18.
m Chap. 19

FINIS.

ERRATA.

[These have been applied to the text.]

www.ingramcontent.com/pod-product-compliance
Lightning Source LLC
Chambersburg PA
CBHW032242080426
42735CB00008B/960